Spiritual Warfare

Spiritual Warfare

A BIBLICAL AND BALANCED PERSPECTIVE

Brian S. Borgman
and
Rob Ventura

Reformation Heritage Books
Grand Rapids, Michigan

Reformation Heritage Books
2965 Leonard St. NE
Grand Rapids, MI 49525
616-977-0889 / Fax 616-285-3246
orders@heritagebooks.org
www.heritagebooks.org

Printed in the United States of America
14 15 16 17 18 19/10 9 8 7 6 5 4 3 2 1

Library of Congress Cataloging-in-Publication Data

Borgman, Brian.
  Spiritual warfare : a biblical and balanced perspective / Brian S. Borgman and Rob Ventura.
     pages cm
  ISBN 978-1-60178-284-7 (pbk. : alk. paper) 1. Spiritual warfare. I. Title.
  BV4509.5.B66 2014
  235'.4—dc23
                        2013042433

For additional Reformed literature, request a free book list from Reformation Heritage Books at the above regular or e-mail address.

Contents

Foreword

The Christian life is not a playground. Rather, it is a battlefield of spiritual warfare. The closer we follow the Lord Jesus Christ, the more we advance to the front line of the conflict. This is the sobering reality that confronts every believer. No Christian can afford to be ignorant of the threatening schemes of spiritual combat, not when so dangerous an enemy is seeking the destruction of our faith. It is critical that we be well informed regarding Satan, who prowls about as a roaring lion seeking someone to devour.

There are three formidable foes with which we contend—the world, the flesh, and the devil. *The world* refers to the evil system around us that is opposed to God. *The flesh* is our old nature that is likewise opposed to God and can do nothing to please Him. *The devil* is a fallen angel who presides over the kingdom of darkness. Satan's strategy is to use the world and the flesh to throw our Christian lives into devastation. The moment a person is converted to Christ, he begins to meet opposition from the devil in his Christian life. His faith is constantly under attack. No believer is exempt from this warfare as a conscientious objector who can escape being drafted. Every disciple of Christ is thrown into this arena of conflict.

It is for this reason that I am grateful for this book, *Spiritual Warfare: A Biblical and Balanced Perspective*, by Brian Borgman and Rob Ventura. These two authors have done an excellent job of expounding Ephesians 6:10–20 regarding what every Christian must implement as one enlisted into active service. With theological precision and pastoral care, Borgman and Ventura carefully handle the biblical text as they apply this key passage to the lives of their readers. I believe you will be greatly profited by this book as you read it—and more than that, live it.

May the Lord use this work for the strengthening of believers as they wrestle against the forces of darkness. To God be the glory for the decisive victory He gives to His faithful soldiers.

Soli Deo Gloria,
Steven J. Lawson
senior pastor
Christ Fellowship Baptist Church
Mobile, Alabama

Preface

If we were on a battlefield in Iraq or Afghanistan and forgot we were in war, we would be dead in no time. Awareness and vigilance are critical for survival. It is sad that we, as followers of Jesus, so easily forget that we are in a war—an invisible war, but a real one nonetheless.

This book is the effort of two pastors who want to remind the church of this war. It is our desire to help Christians to be equipped and to think and fight biblically in a practical way. What would our churches and families look like if we took the spiritual fight seriously? What would our marriages look like if we remembered that our battle is not against flesh and blood? What would our evangelism look like if we were wide-awake to the battle that rages? It is our prayer that the Holy Spirit will use this book to encourage and equip the church to be strong in the Lord and the power of His might.

— Brian Borgman

My good friend and mentor, Pastor Jim Domm, always says, "The Christian life is like standing on the head of a pin. You can easily fall off in any direction." As a pastor who believes these words to be true, I have always tried to expound various biblical subjects with proportionate theological precision in order to assist God's people in being spiritually balanced in their walk with the Lord.

One subject in the Word of God that individuals have often handled with imbalance is the topic of spiritual warfare. While teachers on the subject have emphasized certain elements, unfortunately, they have frequently omitted key components, leaving Christians either ill equipped or ignorant for this great fight of all fights. I pray that what I have contributed to this book accurately reflects the whole counsel of God to the end that His great Name may be praised and His people genuinely helped on their way to heaven.

— Rob Ventura

Acknowledgments

Brian Borgman
A Nevadan and a Rhode Islander (originally a Long Islander) collaborating on a book is a display of the diversity in the body of Christ! I thank Rob Ventura for his love and enthusiasm for Christ and His people and their good, as evidenced by his contribution to this book.

I thank God for the faithful saints of Grace Community Church, who love Christ, His Word, and one another. Remember, we are in this battle together!

To my fellow elders: I thank God that we fight side by side in prayer and the ministry of the Word.

I also want to thank my former professor Clinton Arnold, who was one of the first to teach me how serious this war is.

To my wife, Ariel, also known as Wonder Woman, I am proud of you and thankful that I am in this battle with you.

I affectionately dedicate this book to my parents, Steve and Linda Borgman, who were in Christ before me. I love both of you and thank God for you.

Rob Ventura
Brian, it has been a joy coauthoring this book with you. Working with you and learning from what you have written have truly blessed my soul.

Jack Buckley, my co-pastor: Thanks for all that you do to make my writing the best it can be. Your work is outstanding and has been a true help to me.

In addition, I want to thank D. Scott Meadows and my son Joshua Ventura, who both had a part in making very valuable edits to my rough drafts. I greatly thank you for your diligent labors.

Thank you, Rob Freire, for reading through the entire manuscript and making excellent changes and corrections throughout. Your attention to detail is much appreciated.

Dr. Robert Burrelli, Michael Ives, Jim Sole, Tony Vuolo, and Mark Slater read the entire final draft and provided helpful feedback. Brothers, I thank you for taking time out of your busy schedules to do this.

To the congregation that I pastor in Rhode Island, Grace Community Baptist Church: What I have contributed to this book comes from a series of consecutive expository sermons that I preached to you on the subject at hand. Thank you for your warm reception of that material.

Special thanks to Reformation Heritage Books. Your commitment to the Word of God and to publishing Christ-centered, God-honoring literature makes collaborating a true delight. Particular thanks to Dr. Joel Beeke, Jay Collier, Steve Renkema, David Woollin, and Annette Gysen. You are all dear co-laborers in the Lord.

Finally, my cherished family: I thank you for freely sacrificing your time with me so that I could write this book. I love you all very much.

I dedicate this book to all of the spiritual soldiers in Jesus' army throughout the world. Continue to fight the good fight of faith knowing that "the God of peace will crush Satan under your feet shortly. The grace of our Lord Jesus Christ be with you. Amen" (Rom. 16:20).

One Side of the Horse or the Other

Living the Christian life is not merely about mastering one truth or even a set of principles. Rather, it is learning to think and act biblically. We must be reminded of certain truths frequently so that we don't become unbalanced or myopic in our view of the Christian life. One such truth is that we are in a war of the most serious nature, and that war is not with flesh and blood but against spiritual forces of darkness. This vital truth ought to shape our worldview. Unfortunately, some Christians almost completely ignore the reality of this war. Others, however, seem to give it far more attention than Scripture does. There is certainly a danger in both extremes. C. S. Lewis makes precisely this point in his famous work *The Screwtape Letters*: "There are two equal and opposite errors into which our race can fall about the devils. One is to disbelieve in their existence. The other is to believe, and to feel an excessive and unhealthy interest in them. They themselves are equally pleased by both errors and hail a materialist or a magician with the same delight."[1] Making a similar observation, Martin Luther once noted that Christians are often like a drunk trying to get on his horse. First, the drunk falls off one side, only to climb back up and fall off the other side. Given the stakes in this war, we cannot afford to fall off either side.

---

1. C. S. Lewis, preface to *The Screwtape Letters* (New York: MacMillan Company, 1944), 9.

THE TWO EXTREMES

Since the eighteenth-century Enlightenment, the worldview of the West has grown increasingly closed to the supernatural. Consequently, many people today deny a world that God governs in which the devil and his demons are our enemies. This worldview is called *naturalism*. In this view, everything has a natural cause, and nothing exists beyond what we can see with our eyes. The biblical worldview, however, clashes with naturalism and not only embraces a sovereign God who rules over His world and the events of our lives but also acknowledges Satan and demons. As Christians, we might have a biblical worldview in certain areas, but perhaps our perspective is more naturalistic than we realize. When we adopt this perspective, we view the universe as closed and leave little room for the supernatural. Although we may give credence to God's providence, the spiritual and supernatural do not factor in much in the way we view everyday life.

In contrast, proponents of the other extreme treat spiritual warfare as the lens through which they perceive everything. Those who hold to this view attribute virtually everything that happens to demonic activity and spiritual warfare. This worldview is built more upon fictional books and movies than the Bible. David Powlison notes, "A great deal of fiction, superstition, fantasy, nonsense, nuttiness, and downright heresy flourishes in the church under the guise of 'spiritual warfare' in our time."[2]

Some false teachings include demon-possessed Christians,[3] formulas for exorcisms, binding the devil,[4] rebuking demons, and mapping their physical location. Many of these ideas have little or no biblical foundation; in fact, in the central New Testament passage

---

2. David Powlison, *Power Encounters: Reclaiming Spiritual Warfare* (Grand Rapids: Baker, 1995), 13.

3. See appendix 2 of this book for a discussion of whether Christians can be demon-possessed.

4. In Ephesians 6:11, the apostle Paul writes, "Put on the whole armor of God, that you may be able to stand against the wiles of the devil." If we could bind the devil, why would Paul call us to put on the whole armor of God to stand against him?

on spiritual warfare (Eph. 6:10–20), the apostle Paul makes no mention of any of these things. What they all lack is solid scriptural footing, and while many people throughout the ages have attempted to build doctrinal skyscrapers on such chicken coop foundations, these structures inevitably fall under their own weight. Their end is like that of the man who builds his house upon the sand, only to have it destroyed by rain, floods, and wind (Matt. 7:25–27). The personal ramifications are tragic.

Doctrinal excesses like those just described often lead to an imbalance in the Christian life that magnifies one aspect of biblical truth to the minimization or exclusion of the rest of Scripture. These imbalances often result in the eclipsing or ignoring of such biblical truths as the believer's responsibility for his or her own actions, remaining sin in the Christian, the character-changing power of the Spirit, and the centrality of the gospel. The danger here is not that we might neglect spiritual warfare but that we develop a truncated view of the Christian life in which we wrongly blame Satan and demons for every problem we face. If we are to live sound and stable lives as believers, then we desperately need a biblically balanced understanding of spiritual realities and the spiritual warfare to which God calls us. Anything else will be disastrous.

THE BIBLICAL HISTORY OF SPIRITUAL WARFARE

Spiritual warfare has existed from the beginning of human history. The events leading to the fall of Adam in the garden were the inception of the battle.[5] Satan twisted God's Word, challenged His authority, and lied to our first parents. After the fall, God promised continued warfare and ultimate victory. God said to the serpent,

---

5. Such passages as Isaiah 14:12–14; Ezekiel 28:12–19; Luke 10:18; Jude 6; and Revelation 12:9–12 seem to indicate that the devil was originally created as a perfect angelic being that dwelt in heaven with God, yet was removed from this lofty estate with a third of his angels because of their rebellion. For further discussion of this topic, see Wayne Grudem's *Systematic Theology* (Grand Rapids: Zondervan, 1994), 412–14.

> And I will put enmity
> Between you and the woman,
> And between your seed and her Seed;
> He shall bruise your head,
> And you shall bruise His heel. (Gen. 3:15)

The struggle between the serpent and the woman would continue with their seed. Finally, the serpent would have a bruised head (a fatal blow), and the seed of the woman would have a bruised heel (an injury), but not permanently. Theologians call this the *protoeuangelion*, "the first gospel." The seed of the woman is ultimately Jesus Christ. Although there would be a battle between those who follow Satan, such as Cain, and those who follow God, such as Abel (1 John 3:10–12), and there would be a battle between Satan and those who follow Jesus (1 Peter 5:8; Rev. 12:6–17), the ultimate battle would be between Satan and Christ (Rev. 12:1–5). Part of Christ's mission when He came to earth was to overthrow the work of the kingdom of darkness.

> But Jesus knew their thoughts, and said to them: "Every kingdom divided against itself is brought to desolation, and every city or house divided against itself will not stand. If Satan casts out Satan, he is divided against himself. How then will his kingdom stand? And if I cast out demons by Beelzebub, by whom do your sons cast them out? Therefore they shall be your judges. But if I cast out demons by the Spirit of God, surely the kingdom of God has come upon you. Or how can one enter a strong man's house and plunder his goods, unless he first binds the strong man? And then he will plunder his house." (Matt. 12:25–29)

Every time Jesus cast out a demon, healed the sick, or raised the dead, He was assaulting the kingdom of darkness. Jesus was entering the strong man's house, binding him with His superior strength, and plundering his stolen property. We see this, for example, when He freed the woman who had a demonically induced disability for eighteen years. The synagogue ruler objected to the healing since it was on the Sabbath; however, Jesus responded, "Ought not this woman, being a daughter of Abraham, whom Satan has bound—think of it—for eighteen years, be loosed from this bond on the Sabbath?" (Luke 13:16).

Jesus' ultimate overthrow of Satan, however, took place at the cross. Certainly, the work of Jesus on the cross is multifaceted. There are so many dimensions to His redemptive work that we cannot narrow it to one truth. However, one aspect that we cannot overlook is that at the cross, Jesus was stripping Satan of his power and performing the ultimate rescue operation.

> Now My soul is troubled, and what shall I say? "Father, save Me from this hour"? But for this purpose I came to this hour. Father, glorify Your name.
>
> Then a voice came from heaven, saying, "I have both glorified it and will glorify it again."
>
> Therefore the people who stood by and heard it said that it had thundered. Others said, "An angel has spoken to Him."
>
> Jesus answered and said, "This voice did not come because of Me, but for your sake. Now is the judgment of this world; now the ruler of this world will be cast out." (John 12:27–31)

The cross was an act of judgment evicting the ruler of this world. Years later, the apostle John would reflect on the incarnation and death of Jesus with these words: "For this purpose the Son of God was manifested, that He might destroy the works of the devil" (1 John 3:8). According to John, this means that part of our salvation experience is deliverance from Satan's power and kingdom.

> Having disarmed principalities and powers, He made a public spectacle of them, triumphing over them in it. (Col. 2:15)

> Inasmuch then as the children have partaken of flesh and blood, He Himself likewise shared in the same, that through death He might destroy him who had the power of death, that is, the devil, and release those who through fear of death were all their lifetime subject to bondage. (Heb. 2:14–15)

Now, as followers of Jesus, we live in the tension of the "already" and the "not yet" (a subject we will discuss in detail in chapter 2). That is, we have been delivered from Satan's dominion through the finished work of Christ, yet we still battle. Part of our struggle in this life is that we must fight against Satan and his forces in the world. One day our victory in Christ will be fully realized: "The God of peace will crush Satan under your feet shortly" (Rom. 16:20). But until that time, we must keep in mind the following truth: we are wrestling not against human beings but spiritual powers (Eph. 6:12). Scripture commands us, therefore, to be alert because our enemy the devil is seeking to devour us (1 Peter 5:8).

How we think about this battle is critical to how we fight it. We cannot emphasize enough the significance of Ephesians 6:10–20, which is the basis of this book. This classic passage gives us a biblical framework for spiritual warfare. On the one hand, it frees us from the misconception of a closed, naturalistic worldview that understates our spiritual battle. On the other hand, it provides us with a sane approach that avoids overstating it as well. This text gives us a perspective on spiritual warfare that can dramatically shape our daily lives, showing us how to engage rightly in this great war.

Our approach in this book is straightforward. We will present what Paul says about fighting this fight in Ephesians 6:10–20. Along the way, we will explain each piece of armor and practically apply its truth to our lives. Our primary focus will not be Satan, but Christ, who is the victor over all.

FOR REFLECTION AND DISCUSSION

1. When we consider the subject of spiritual warfare, what are the two extremes we need to avoid? Why might we gravitate toward either of the extremes?

2. How have you fallen off the horse on one side or the other (as Martin Luther put it)? What truths will keep you from falling off?

3. What do you find encouraging about the history of this spiritual war?

4. What area of your thinking or living was directly challenged by this history?

CHAPTER 1

Be Strong in the Lord

*Finally, my brethren, be strong in the Lord and in the
power of His might.*
— EPHESIANS 6:10

Our first step in successfully waging spiritual warfare is recognizing our weakness and the Lord's great strength. Self-sufficiency is a killer in this battle; dependence on Christ is crucial. Ephesians 6:10–20 repeatedly reminds us of our insufficiency for this fight. We need strength (v. 10), weaponry (vv. 11; 14–17), and lines of communication with our Savior for aid (vv. 18–20). These means are external to us. Without them, we have inadequate strength to stand against principalities, powers, the rulers of the darkness, and spiritual hosts of wickedness. Left to ourselves we would soon crumble in the heat of battle. We are simply deficient for the task. However, God loves His people and never leaves them defenseless.

As we now consider Ephesians 6:10, attempting to clarify its meaning and apply its truths, let's consider this verse in its overall context. The book of Ephesians divides neatly into two parts. The first is a doctrinal foundation, and the second builds on that foundation with practical application of those doctrines to the life of the church. This follows Paul's typical pattern in his writings: the indicative (a declaration of what God has done in Christ) followed by the imperative (what we are to do in response). Paul's practical application begins in Ephesians 4:1 and reaches its climax in 6:10–20, a cosmic perspective on the Christian life with the believer engaged in spiritual warfare.

As Paul draws his letter to a close, he begins this new section with the word finally. We should find it interesting that the crowning section of the epistle, this grand finale, focuses on spiritual warfare. It is significant that the apostle cannot end this letter, which he has filled with so many magnificent truths, without instructing his readers about the great ongoing threat they face. In order for us to understand why he ends on this note, we need to know something about the Ephesians and their city, Ephesus.

EPHESUS, THE SPIRITUAL CITY

Ephesus was a thriving metropolis on the west coast of Asia Minor, ranking alongside Rome and Alexandria as a major Roman city. According to legend, Amazons (giant female warriors) founded the city. This well-known legend influenced Ephesian culture religiously and socially. The population of Ephesus was estimated at more than 250,000 in the first century, which made it the third largest city in the empire. An advanced city, it boasted an amphitheater that held twenty-four thousand people, baths, gymnasiums, and a medical training school. It also hosted the *Koina Asias*, the common games of Asia. Beyond its sophistication and technological development, it was also a spiritual city. The chief religion of Ephesus was the cult of Artemis Ephesia (Greek name) or Diana of Ephesus (Roman name).

The Artemis cult was predominant throughout Asia Minor. The *Artemosian*, the temple that housed the multibreasted figure of Artemis, was constructed of marble and measured 93,500 square feet. Each of its 127 marble columns stood sixty feet high. The temple was one of the seven wonders of the ancient world. Clinton Arnold explains, "The worshipers of Artemis extolled their goddess as supreme in power, a 'cosmic' power that was believed to be superior to that of any other deity, astrological fate, and evil spirits."[1]

---

1. Clinton E. Arnold, *Ephesians Power and Magic: The Concept of Power in Ephesians in Light of Its Historical Context* (Grand Rapids: Baker, 1992), 39.

Ephesus was also the center for magical practices. Bruce Metzger notes, "Of all ancient Greco-Roman cities, Ephesus was by far the most hospitable to magicians, sorcerers, and charlatans of all sorts."[2] The famous *Ephesia Grammata* (Ephesian letters) were words written on amulets that the people used as charms, believing that they brought protection from the powers (evil spirits) or gave them help in times of distress or need. Furthermore, Jewish involvement in power and magic was pervasive.[3]

When Paul arrived in Ephesus, an event recorded in Acts 19, he found a metropolis trafficking in the occult and the powers of darkness. The Ephesians lived with a worldview that was completely open to supernaturalism. Magic, demons, and spiritual power were very real to them, and many were involved in occult practices. Paul ministered there for three months in the synagogue and two years in the school of Tyrannus (Acts 19:8–10). During this time, the word of the Lord was shining forth in Ephesian darkness. Many were coming to faith in Jesus and repenting of their sorceries: "And many who had believed came confessing and telling their deeds. Also, many of those who had practiced magic brought their books together and burned them in the sight of all. And they counted up the value of them, and it totaled fifty thousand pieces of silver. So the word of the Lord grew mightily and prevailed" (Acts 19:18–20).

In Ephesus, the gospel began to have a serious impact on the religious scene. The city was so deeply committed to Diana, both religiously and commercially, that when people were converted and stopped buying idols, a riot broke out because of the loss of revenue (Acts 19:21–41). This riot happened just as Paul was planning to leave the city. By this time he had ministered three years among these Ephesian believers (Acts 20:31). He knew them well, and he knew their struggles. Since it is common for believers to deeply

---

2. Quoted in Arnold, *Ephesians Power and Magic*, 14.

3. Dr. Clinton Arnold, a leading New Testament scholar and expert on Ephesian spirituality, has detailed these practices. Arnold's *Ephesians Power and Magic* is his academic work on the subject; *Powers of Darkness* (Downers Grove, Ill.: InterVarsity, 1992) is his popular treatment of the subject.

regret their wicked lives before Christ rescued them, it could be that their occultist pasts were haunting some converted Ephesians. Perhaps they even lived in fear of the spiritual powers with which they had been acquainted.

As we come to Ephesians 6:10–20, we see that the apostle does not dismiss the realities of the powers, like a parent reassuring a child that there really is not a monster under his bed. Rather, he validates spiritual realities and equips the believers for the battle at hand.

SUMMARY EXHORTATION: "BE STRONG IN THE LORD"

Paul's command to "be strong" means literally "be strengthened, or be made powerful." Paul has good reason to begin this section of his letter this way. As soldiers in Jesus' army, we will face many battles and hardships on our way to heaven. At times, we will feel besieged and utterly exhausted. We will keenly feel temptation and suffer battle wounds. Therefore, we must be provoked to pursue spiritual strength and power. A feeble or cowardly disposition in spiritual warfare will be detrimental to our success. It will cause us to regress. In light of this, Paul calls us to be mighty men. He wants us to enter this battle courageously and with great hope. This call to be strong is a constant one in Scripture. As Joshua was commanded to "be strong and of good courage," or to be "very courageous" (Josh. 1:6, 7, 9) and David "strengthened himself in the LORD his God" (1 Sam. 30:6), we must do the same.[4] If we would triumph in our walk with Christ as we engage in spiritual battle, we must seriously heed this exhortation.

Paul's charge to "be strong" is in the passive voice in the original Greek, which means that this empowering is something that is done to us from an outside source. This tells us that we dare not look to ourselves for strength in this combat. We do not draw stamina for spiritual battle from within or by flexing our muscles from without. Rather, Paul calls us specifically to be "strong *in the Lord*." Here is

---

4. In addition to these references, see 1 Corinthians 16:13 and 2 Timothy 2:1.

where we find our strength—in the Son of God Himself. What a glorious thought! Paul points us to Christ as the all-sufficient source of our strength, who, by His mighty power, gives us all that we lack. As believers we can do all things through Christ who strengthens us (Phil. 4:13).

But there are other nuggets of truth in these words. The command "be strong" is also in the present tense, indicating that in Christ we have constant, ongoing supplies of all that we need for spiritual warfare. Jesus is our continual refuge and strength, our very present help in trouble (Ps. 46:1).

Yet what does it mean to be strong in the Lord? In summary, it means to maintain an ongoing awareness that the Lord Jesus has superabundant stores of strength for us, and, as we realize this, we draw from that strength continuously. The idea is that by virtue of our union with Christ, we utilize the strength that is inherent in Him. Our Lord has all we need for warfare. Though we are weak, He is strong, and He perfects His strength in our weakness (2 Cor. 12:9). Therefore, as the battle rages on, we are to look to Him for help, for His "divine power has given to us all things that pertain to life and godliness" (2 Peter 1:3).

Paul consistently reminded the Ephesians that the power of God in Christ was available to them, so it should not be surprising that he now calls them to make good use of it. This power is nothing less than the power of Jesus Christ demonstrated in His resurrection and exaltation (Eph. 1:19–20). Since we have been raised with Him and are seated with Him (Eph. 2:6), that power is ours in Him.

We do well to pause and ask ourselves if we are persuaded of this reality concerning our Lord. How we view Him will be a major factor in our regularly going to Him to "obtain mercy and find grace to help in time of need" (Heb. 4:16). Never forget that Jesus is no longer the Suffering Servant of Jehovah dying on the cross. Rather, He is the exalted King of heaven and earth reigning on high (1 Cor. 15:20–25)! Jesus is the risen Head of the church who fills "all in all" (Eph. 1:23). He is the One in whom dwells "all the fullness of the Godhead bodily" (Col. 2:9). We are not to file these truths about Christ in some dusty theological cabinet. Instead, they are to prod us to action. This knowledge about our Lord is to drive us to the One who is able to do exceedingly abundantly above all that we ask or think. It should remind us that the weapons of our warfare are not carnal but mighty in God for pulling down strongholds (2 Cor. 10:4). So avail yourself of this power in Christ (Eph. 3:20–21). Daily cast all your cares upon Him, for He cares for you (1 Peter 5:7).

In Ephesians 6:10, the phrase "and in the power of His might" amplifies and expands what it means to be strong in the Lord. These words take us back to Ephesians 1:17–23, where Paul describes his prayer for the Ephesians:

> that the God of our Lord Jesus Christ, the Father of glory, may give to you the spirit of wisdom and revelation in the knowledge of Him, the eyes of your understanding being enlightened; that you may know what is the hope of His calling, what are the riches of the glory of His inheritance in the saints, and what is the exceeding greatness of His power toward us who believe, according to the working of His mighty power which He worked in Christ when He raised Him from the dead and seated Him at His right hand in the heavenly places, far above all principality and power and might and dominion, and every name that is named, not only in this age but also in that which is to come.
>
> And He put all things under His feet, and gave Him to be head over all things to the church, which is His body, the fullness of Him who fills all in all.

Here we see Christ's unrivaled power in His resurrection, ascension, and exaltation. No other power compares with it, and Christ is its great focal point. The Father exerted this divine power in raising Christ from the dead, thereby destroying the inferior power of death. This divine power was subsequently exerted in Christ's enthronement, resulting in His being seated at the Father's "right hand in the heavenly places" (1:20). The right hand is the place of honor, power, victory, and authority. Christ Himself is far above "all principality and power and might and dominion" (1:21). Paul uses these terms to refer to evil spiritual powers in Ephesians 6:12. Christ is also surpassingly above "every name that is named" (1:21). Here, Paul includes those names the unsaved Ephesians invoked in their incantations to harness spiritual powers. The central message of the apostle here is clear: Christ is higher than and far superior to all powers that exist, including every demonic and spiritual power!

Christ as the exalted and enthroned Lord rules over all. The entire spirit world is subject to Him, "not only in this age but also in that which is to come" (1:21). Jesus inaugurated the age to come at His first advent. He will consummate the age to come at His second advent. Christ will reign in the age to come. However, He presently reigns in this age. Murray Harris notably says, "The resurrection proclaims 'He lives—and that forever'; the exaltation proclaims 'He reigns—and that forever.'"

Jesus' resurrection, exaltation, and reign demonstrate the surpassing power vested in His person, and this power is already ours in Him. This is what the apostle says he wants us to be aware of in Ephesians 1:18–23. This omnipotent power conquers all the spiritual forces of every age. There is nothing lacking in it. This power alone will see us through our battles with the devil.

If we have been injured in spiritual battle, we should ask ourselves if we have been relying on the power we possess in Christ. In and of ourselves, we are not fit for this great fight. We do not have the necessary strength or skill to oppose Satan and spiritual forces. We are not as strong as we think; sadly, our experience confirms this. Nevertheless, in spiritual union with the risen Lord, we have His infinite power and strength by faith. Ephesians 6:10 calls us, then, to be humble, dependent warriors constantly going to Christ, the captain of our salvation, for this mighty power. It calls us to recognize our native deficiency and to see His great spiritual sufficiency. This is the essence of Paul's opening exhortation. Charles Hodge put it this way: "He, therefore, who rushes into this conflict without thinking of Christ, without putting his trust in him, and without continually looking to him for strength, and regarding himself as a member of his body, deriving all life and vigour from him, *is demented*.... When we are weak, then are we strong. When most empty of self, we are most full of God."[5]

FOR REFLECTION AND DISCUSSION

1. What parallels do you see between ancient Ephesus and the society in which you live today?

2. In your own words, describe how Ephesians 1:18–21 is relevant for you in your daily battle.

3. The authors say, "Self-sufficiency is a killer in this battle." Explain how you can fall into a pattern of self-sufficiency. Discuss why this is dangerous and how you can cultivate dependence upon the Lord.

4. Because of all that Christ has gained for us in His life, death, resurrection, and exaltation, what should our attitude be as we engage in spiritual warfare?

---

5. Charles Hodge, *Ephesians* (1856; repr., Edinburgh: Banner of Truth, 1991), 275–76.

CHAPTER 2

Put On the Full Armor of God

Put on the whole armor of God, that you may be able to stand...
— EPHESIANS 6:11

Jesus Christ's cross and resurrection spelled Satan's doom. Christ's second advent will seal Satan's doom—and sin and death with him. We Christians live between the resurrection and the second coming, the time when Christ has freed us from Satan's dominion, yet spiritual powers still attack us. Our ultimate victory is sure because of all that our Savior has done and will do for us when He returns. Nevertheless, we are still in a real war fighting real enemies and encountering real casualties.

As we mentioned in the introduction, we live between the "already" and the "not yet." As we saw in the last chapter, Jesus, through His death, resurrection, ascension, and reign, inaugurated the age to come. That is the "already." The "not yet" awaits His second advent, when He will consummate all things in the new heaven and the new earth and put a complete end to Satan and his work. Practically speaking, this means that life between the "already" and the "not yet" is a life of tension between what we must now do as Christian soldiers and what Jesus will do when He appears.

In Ephesians 6, the apostle Paul is equipping us to live between Christ's first and second coming. He is revealing the resources we need in order to repel the assaults of the enemy while we live between these two grand stages of redemptive history. We will see in this chapter—and in the rest of this book—that Paul understood that we Christians need further explanations and applications on what it means to be filled with strength from the Lord if we are to be good soldiers skilled in the use of arms. According to Paul, we must put on armor, train for war, and prepare for the day of battle.

THE CALL TO PUT ON THE ARMOR

The action in verse 11, to "put on" or "clothe yourselves" with the whole armor of God, figuratively describes a person putting on spiritual or ethical qualities like a garment. As we begin to take a closer look at what this means, we will take a slight detour. In his writings, Paul frequently uses the imagery of "being clothed" or "putting on" within the context of our new life in Christ. This is an important fact, and we must not miss it. Paul tells us in Galatians 3:27 that we were already *clothed* in Christ when we were baptized into Him. Elsewhere he tells us that, in contrast to living like the lost, we need to *put on* the new man (Eph. 4:24; Col. 3:10). In Colossians 3:12 he says that as the elect of God, we are to *put on* "tender mercies, kindness, humility, meekness, longsuffering."

All this teaches us that being clothed with Christ is our new identity and realm of life as Christians. This is a redemptive reality for us that relates directly to our being fully clothed with God's covering. The point is, as we regularly put on Christ as we are commanded (Rom. 13:14), we become well suited for spiritual warfare. Apart from Christ we can do nothing (John 15:5), and as we live connected to and conscious of our oneness, association, and identification with Him, we will be fully clad with all the virtue of His blessed person.

As we turn our focus back to Ephesians 6, let's keep in mind this big picture about donning spiritual armor. We will soon unpack each individual piece, but understand at this point that wearing spiritual armor is an essential element of putting on Christ and applying the new life of grace in Him; it is not something separate. Putting on God's armor is taking what God has so richly supplied in His Son and appropriating it personally each day. When we put on God's armor, we are doing more than applying a technique or method. We are doing something personal; we are putting on Christ

Himself. Since Christ is all-sufficient, everything that we need to be covered is found in Him. All *truth* is connected to Him (John 14:6). All *righteousness* has its source in Him (1 Cor. 1:30). He is the central subject of *the gospel of peace,* for He is our peace (Eph. 2:14)—and so on through the list (6:14–17). Clinton Arnold explains that, therefore, "knowing the truth of who we are in union with Christ, cultivating the virtues of this new identity, and using the resources available through this new relationship are at the heart of what it means to put on the armor of God."[1]

Nevertheless, putting on the whole armor is also an ethical responsibility. We must live according to our new identity and walk in the sphere of our new existence. When Paul tells us to put on the whole armor of God, he is using this vivid metaphor to convey how we must do it. He is spelling out for us how we gain spiritual strength from the Lord, that same astounding strength he spoke of in Ephesians 6:10. To do this means that we must make God's spiritual armor an integral part of our entire being. It means that we must constantly call to mind who we are in Christ so that we avoid walking around exposed and defenseless against the evil one. In short, we adopt the mind-set of a serious soldier. This is how we will be well protected.

Notice that the apostle commands us to put on the *whole* armor of God. The whole armor implies the full combat gear of a well-equipped soldier. Paul enlarges upon these words later in this passage as he describes our spiritual weaponry in detail in verses 14 through 17. As Christians, we need the whole armor because our enemy is a relentless foe. If Satan cannot wound us in one place, he will target another: if not the head, then the heart; if not the conscience, then the emotions. Since Satan attacks us in a variety of ways, God provides a variety of defenses sufficient to withstand any assault he might throw at us. In Christ, God grants us all that we need to protect us from head to toe.

---

1. Clinton E. Arnold, *Exegetical Commentary on the New Testament* (Grand Rapids: Zondervan, 2010), 444.

In a sermon titled "Shoes for Pilgrims and Warriors," Charles Spurgeon highlights our need to wear the whole armor of God at all times:

> [Satan] will attack you sometimes by force and sometimes by fraud. By might or by sleight he will seek to overcome you and no unarmed man can stand against him. Never go out without all your armor on, for you can never tell where you may meet the devil. He is not omnipresent, but nobody can tell where he is not, for he and his troops of devils appear to be found everywhere on this earth.[2]

D. Martyn Lloyd-Jones echoes this point:

> This again is something of crucial importance. It means that we do not pick and choose this matter. If you are to be a soldier in this army, if you are to fight victoriously in this crusade, you have to put on the entire equipment given to you. That is a rule in any army. You cannot select which parts of your uniform you are going to put on. If you say, "I do not think this is going to suit me, I do not quite like that," you know exactly what will happen to you. And that is infinitely more true in this spiritual realm and warfare with which we are concerned. The moment you begin to say, "I need this helmet but I do not need this breastplate," you are already defeated. You need it all—"the *whole* armor of God"—because your understanding is inadequate. It is God alone who knows your enemy, and he knows exactly the provision that is essential to you if you are to continue standing. Every single part and portion of this armor is absolutely essential; and the first thing you have to learn is that you are not in a position to pick and choose.[3]

Moreover, we must observe that we are to put on the whole armor *of God*.[4] God Himself is the source of this armor. He is the

---

2. C. H. Spurgeon, "Shoes for Pilgrims and Warriors," *Metropolitan Tabernacle Pulpit* no. 3143, http://www.spurgeongems.org/vols55–57/chs3143.pdf.

3. D. Martyn Lloyd-Jones, *The Christian Soldier* (Grand Rapids: Baker 1977), 179.

4. For a discussion on this phrase in the original language, we point the reader to Peter O'Brien, *The Letter to the Ephesians*, The Pillar New Testament Commentary Series (Grand Rapids: Eerdmans, 1999), 463.

one who supplies it; we do not supply it ourselves. We should also note that the concept of God's armor was not Paul's newfangled idea; rather, it is rooted in the Old Testament. The Old Testament depicts Jesus the Messiah as the ultimate warrior, fighting and winning the ultimate war for His people. Isaiah 11:4–5 and 59:16–17 picture Christ as clothed in God's armor. In addition, various pieces of the Divine Warrior's armor are an attribute or activity of God Himself (truth, righteousness, peace, faithfulness, and salvation). Indeed, then, what we put on for spiritual warfare is the very armor of God. This armor belongs *to* Him, and it comes *from* Him. What encouragement! Since we have God's armor, whatever the devil brings our way will come to naught. Man-made armor fails us in this fight, but God's armor is impregnable. It cannot be defeated.

THE PURPOSE

Having commanded us to be strong in the Lord in verse 10 and to put on the whole armor of God in verse 11, Paul now tells us why we are to do this: that we may be "able to stand." Here again is encouragement for us. Paul says that if we clothe ourselves with what God supplies, we can stand against the adversary of our souls. It is clear from this that the Christian life is not intended to be one of defeat in which the devil is constantly having his way with us. While we might lose some battles with Satan at times, the believer is ultimately the winner because He who is in him is greater than he who is in the world (1 John 4:4). The point is that because we are saved, *we should* stand against the devil. We *must* stand against the devil, and *we can* stand against the devil. This reality is glorious. For God not only provides His people with divinely impenetrable armor, but He also motivates them to wear it by holding out the prospect of success.

This matter of standing might sound a little less spectacular than we expected. Perhaps we think the verse should go something like this: "Put on the whole armor of God so that you can kill the enemy!" Or, "Put on the whole armor of God so that you might topple the powers of darkness, cast out or bind demons, and take dominion!" However, the apostle informs us that the purpose of putting on the armor is simply to stand. The verb *stand* means to hold one's position continually. It suggests a soldier firm and steady while under fierce attack. Thus, Paul is calling us to put on the full armor of God so that the devil will not gain one inch in our lives or lead us off course. Paul's point is that he does not want us to be pushed around by the enemy of our souls. Rather, he wants us to stay on the narrow path that leads to life. When the devil advances, we are to stand, holding our position, employing God's mighty armor and refusing to be moved. Stanley D. Gale says,

> Standing is not passive.... The idea is not to stand around, but to stand firm. It is to stand like an oak against the winds of Satan's lies that would sway us, against the floods of his temptations that would sweep us away, and against the leeches of his accusations that would deprive us of grace. It is to stand rooted and built up in Christ, strengthened in the faith. If our victory is in Christ, then we are to be grounded in Christ, hearing and doing his Word, living in the power of his resurrection, following his example, resting in his victory.[5]

Paul makes the objective clear, reiterating it later on in this section: "Therefore take up the whole armor of God, that you may be able to *withstand* in the evil day, and having done all, to *stand. Stand therefore*" (Eph. 6:13–14, emphasis added).

Resistance is the objective in these encounters.[6] In spiritual warfare, as in all of life, we do not want to be turned back or aside or knocked down. We want to stand; we want to resist that which opposes us. This is consistent with other passages that express the same objective.

> Be sober, be vigilant; because your adversary the devil walks about like a roaring lion, seeking whom he may devour. *Resist*

---

5. Stanley D. Gale, *What Is Spiritual Warfare?* Basics of the Reformed Faith (Phillipsburg, N.J.: P&R, 2008), 20.

6. Clinton Arnold makes the point that "to stand" is not merely defensive and "needs to be expanded to include an offensive dimension to the warfare." *Exegetical Commentary on the New Testament*, 445.

him, steadfast in the faith, knowing that the same sufferings are experienced by your brotherhood in the world. (1 Peter 5:8–9, emphasis added)

Submit to God. *Resist the devil* and he will flee from you. (James 4:7, emphasis added)

How can we stand and resist Satan successfully? First, as we mentioned at the beginning of the chapter, the answer is we stand by understanding the important balance between the "already" and the "not yet." We stand with the knowledge that although our enemy rages, he is defeated. We stand knowing that although he is a roaring lion, he is also a conquered foe. Though at times he growls, his doom is sure, for the Lion of the tribe of Judah is on our side (Rev. 5:5).

We also stand by being clothed in the power of the Lord and in the strength of His might. Because He reigns and we have been clothed with Him, we can stand and fight. We see, then, that we must always maintain a striking balance between our absolute confidence in our victory in Christ and our responsibility to obey God and put on all of His divine spiritual armor, which we will speak more fully about in the coming chapters. These are the perspectives we must always keep before us as followers of Jesus. God has revealed these truths to us so that we will be both optimistic and observant in waging the good warfare all our earthly days.

FOR REFLECTION AND DISCUSSION

1. What do we mean when we talk about the "already" and the "not yet"? How does understanding these two concepts help you in this spiritual war?

2. How do you know that Paul does not want you to be passive in this battle? What specific command does he call you to obey that shows we must do something?

3. When you have lost spiritual ground to the enemy, what happened? Why might it have happened? What would you do differently today to prevent it?

4. What does it mean to stand? How do we stand?

CHAPTER 3

The Schemes of the Devil

...against the wiles of the devil.
— EPHESIANS 6:11

The Christian can stand and be steady in the face of great spiritual opposition. Paul says that we have this ability, and our resolute stance must have an object. He identifies that object when he says that we are to stand against the "wiles of the devil." The Greek word he uses for "wiles," or "schemes," is *methodia*, from which we get our English word *method,* and it suggests craftily planning with the deliberate intent to deceive.[1] John MacArthur says that this word was often used to describe how a wild animal "cunningly stalked and then unexpectedly pounced on its prey."[2] How like Satan this is, relentlessly pursuing, ever probing for weakness or inattention, and then striking when confident of his advantage!

It is clear from Paul's use of this term that the enemy of our souls is continually hatching new plans to oppose and injure us. The plural use of *wiles* also indicates that Satan's pernicious designs are manifold. Thus, Satan tirelessly weaves all manner of malignant

---

1. Paul used this same Greek word in Ephesians 4:14, but it is translated there as *plotting*. In speaking about false teachers (like the devil) who deceive and delude men's souls, he wrote, "that we should no longer be children, tossed to and fro and carried about with every wind of doctrine, by the trickery of men, in the cunning craftiness of deceitful plotting."

2. John MacArthur, *Ephesians,* The MacArthur New Testament Commentary (Chicago: Moody, 1986), 338.

strategies to ensnare us or make us fall. Yet the Christian wearing the whole armor of God can stand against all of them.

In 2 Corinthians 2:10–11 Paul employs a different word for Satan's plans: "Now whom you forgive anything, I also forgive. For if indeed I have forgiven anything, I have forgiven that one for your sakes in the presence of Christ, lest Satan should take advantage of us; for we are not ignorant of his *devices*" (emphasis added). The Greek word here for "devices" can be a generic term for "thought" or "mind." However, it may also be used in a negative sense, meaning "a bad purpose, design, or plot." The point in bringing attention to these two words is to underscore that the devil is not a passive, unthinking foe. Rather, he is actively and intelligently spinning devious tactics together—tactics that we must oppose and of which we must never be ignorant.

KNOW YOUR ENEMY

To dispel ignorance wherever it may exist, we must have a basic working knowledge of Satan's character and his lines of attack against us. As F. F. Bruce says, "To be forewarned about the nature of his wiles is to be forearmed against them."[3] John Piper adds, "A wartime mindset must include shrewd knowledge of enemy tactics."[4]

As God's names reveal something of His beautiful and glorious character, so also the names of our enemy reveal something of his wicked and malevolent character. In this combat, knowledge of our enemy is vital in order to assure victory in battle. The New Testament identifies our foe as the devil more than thirty times. This name means "slanderer" or "accuser." In 1 Peter 5:8, the devil is called "your adversary," indicating that he is our opponent—one who opposes us.

---

3. F. F. Bruce, *The Epistles to the Colossians, to Philemon, and to the Ephesians*, New International Commentary on the New Testament (Grand Rapids: Eerdmans, 1984), 404.

4. John Piper, "A Handbook of Enemy Strategies," *desiringGod*, http://www.desiringgod.org/resource-library/articles/a-handbook-of-enemy-strategies.

In the Old and New Testaments, he is frequently called Satan, which also conveys the idea of an adversary. As Satan, he is the enemy of God and of all who belong to Him. He is also called "the tempter" (Matt. 4:3; 1 Thess. 3:5); the destroyer, or "Apollyon" (Rev. 9:11); and "the evil one" (Matt. 6:13). In addition, he is called the "dragon," the "serpent of old," and a "roaring lion," which reflect his cunning, fierce, and dangerous hostility toward us (1 Peter 5:8; Rev. 12:3; 20:2). Paul calls him "the god of this age" (2 Cor. 4:4) and "the prince of the power of the air" (Eph. 2:2). Jesus calls him "a murderer" and "a liar" (John 8:44) and "the ruler of this world" (John 12:31; 16:11).

Some of these references express how powerful and deceptive he is and that he, to some degree, rules in this world. But how can that be if God is king and sovereign over all things?[5] Frederick Leahy answers this question well. He considers the texts that call Satan "the god of this age" and "the prince of the power of the air" and then asks:

> Do they mean that Satan has received authority to rule over men? Is this world his dominion, prescribed to him by God upon the fall of man? Was he therefore entitled to promise Christ all the kingdoms of the world? In modern Christian literature one frequently finds affirmative answers to these questions, indeed, the most staggering assertions are made respecting Satan's supposed dominion and power. Some speak of him as sovereign of this world, under a divine sentence which has not yet been executed. Or again, it is said that when Satan successfully tempted Adam he wrested the scepter of authority from man and gained the right to rule the human race. Certainly the Bible does not minimize the sinister power of the Evil One who is the prince of the demons and the head of a godless world-order, a power enhanced by the allegiance, witting or unwitting, of sinful men, and accommodated by the corruption of man's heart. But it remains to be asked if Satan is

---

5. For a further discussion of this topic, see appendix 1, "The Sovereignty of God and Satan."

a monarch in some divinely granted domain, or a vanquished foe, an imposter, a liar and a deceiver.

Scripture leaves us in no doubt about the answer to this important question. Though Adam was a steward and trustee of God's creation, Satan had no authority to rule men, for man was never his own master. And therefore there could be no scepter of rule belonging to man which was transferable to Satan after the Fall. God has given Satan no dominion over man. Man is within "the dominion of Satan" (Acts 26:18) only because of his sin. In revolt against God, he aligned himself with Satan. In this sense Satan is his "god" and "prince"; man is a captive in the jurisdiction of darkness (Col. 1:13).[6]

SATAN IS CRAFTY AND SUBTLE

Satan first appeared on the scene in the garden, and Scripture informs us that he was craftier than any beast of the field (Gen. 3:1). His approach was subtle, and his innuendos were clever. Paul would later reiterate these characteristics:

> But I fear, lest somehow, as the serpent *deceived* Eve by *his craftiness,* so your minds may be corrupted from the simplicity that is in Christ.... For such are false apostles, *deceitful workers,* transforming themselves into apostles of Christ. And no wonder! For Satan himself transforms himself into an angel of light. Therefore it is no great thing if his ministers also transform themselves into ministers of righteousness. (2 Cor. 11:3, 13–15, emphasis added)

The devil's craftiness and subtlety have one main goal—deception. We see this tactic in the garden. Satan comes to Eve and asks, "Has God indeed said, 'You shall not eat of every tree of the garden'?" (Gen. 3:1). With a slight suggestion, Satan impugned God's goodness. As he did later with Job, he attempted to lure Eve to

---

6. Frederick S. Leahy, *Satan Cast Out: A Study in Biblical Demonology* (Edinburgh: Banner of Truth, 1975), 23–24.

deny that God was good. One of Satan's most effective weapons is to get us to question or doubt God's goodness.

Satan will often imply or outright charge that God is not good. For example, he can insinuate doubts into the mind of a single woman who turns forty and longs for a husband and children: "If God is for you—if He is good—why aren't you married yet? You are rapidly passing the age of childbearing. Do you really think God is kind?" Satan seeks to capitalize on our trials or tragedies. He can suggest to the mind of the husband and father who just lost his job and health insurance: "God doesn't care about you. If He did He would have saved your job." Satan lets no crisis go to waste. He will try to use pain and disappointment to pry us away from our confidence that God is gracious and cares for us.

Satan's tactic is also to defy God's character by challenging His Word. As a skilled adversary, he does not have only one trick up his sleeve. At times he may simply snatch up the Word when it has been sown (Matt. 13:19). At other times, he may work his deceit in order to get us to doubt or even disbelieve the Word.

Satan can try to persuade us to misapply and misunderstand the Word, and so inoculate people against its proper meaning. A young mother who loved the Lord and knew His Word was encountering various trials. To an outside observer, her trials were not major—like cancer or the death of a spouse—compared to others in the church. They seemed to be the normal trials of a young family who was struggling financially and interpersonally. As her pastor tried to bring comfort from God's Word, she retorted, "You don't understand! I am like Job; you are just like one of Job's counselors!" As he tried to explain that she was not like Job, she took up passage after passage in the book of Job, misconstruing and misapplying text after text, cementing herself in her own point of view. Her pastor's words meant nothing! She had a failsafe way to dismiss what he was saying. Her perspective, as clouded as it was, had the approval of God's own holy Word—at least that is what she thought. She was in a fog, and the enemy was using the misapplied Word to make the fog denser.

The devil twists the Word of God in innumerable ways (Matt. 4:6; 2 Cor. 11:4; 1 Tim. 4:1), and he does this ultimately to get people to reject it. If he can get people to reject the Word outright, he has then made an effective attack on God. But, more often, he twists the Scripture so that God's character is maligned, the person and work of Christ are distorted, God's grace is perverted, and man's sin is misrepresented. Satan also tries to disfigure the Word through false doctrine, so Martin Luther was right when he frequently said, "Satan hates the Word of God more than any other thing."

Satan's principal weapon is falsehood. This too was evident in the garden when he told Eve, "You will not surely die!" God's truth gives and sustains life. Satan's murderous dishonesty kills and destroys. The devil knows how to lie in ways that appeal to our sense of deserving, our sense of worth or lack of worth, and our sense of rights and wrongs. You name it—Satan can lie about it: "You will be truly happy only if you…." Or, "God doesn't want you lonely so…."

COMMON DEVICES

As the father of lies, the devil uses dishonesty against us, but his arsenal is not so limited. He can afflict (Job 1:6–11), hinder (1 Thess. 2:18), steal (Matt. 13:19), tempt (Matt. 4:1), and persecute (Rev. 2:10; 12:13). Sadly, another weapon in his arsenal that he uses against us with great efficiency is our own sins. All personal disobedience to God in our lives is tantamount to the work of the evil one (Eph. 2:1–3). The Bible is clear that there are specific sins that Satan uses and works through for greater advantages against us.

Anger, for example, is one such sin. Unrighteous and unresolved anger can give Satan a place in our lives (Eph. 4:26–27). Anger is a consuming, destructive vice, and Satan often uses it to gain spiritual ground on us; therefore, we must confess and repent of it.

Satan can also use the related sin of being unforgiving. Paul explicitly makes that point in 2 Corinthians 2:10–11. Being unforgiving is ugly and not at all Christlike. We must deal with this evil through much prayer, because if it continues in us, it will diminish the cross, eclipse grace, harden our heart, and cause great division among the brethren.

Sexual sin is another favorite device Satan uses against us (1 Cor. 7:5). Sexual immorality is deceptive and enslaving. It is grievous (1 Cor. 6:15) and brings guilt, as we see in David's sin with Bathsheba (Ps. 32:3–4). Those who become ensnared in sexual sin lose their ability to grasp God's truth and to walk in it (Prov. 5:22–23; 7:6–7, 21–23), so we must flee from it immediately (1 Cor. 6:18).

In addition to these sins, our pride (Satan's own sin) is often something that he uses against us (1 Tim. 3:6). Scripture forbids pride (Rom. 12:3); it is a great hindrance to our seeking God (Ps. 10:4). In fact, it puts us in opposition to God (James 4:6). Pride is also an enormous impediment to our repentance. It is self-deceptive and self-inflating. How can we possibly submit to and do what God requires of us from His Word when our hearts are filled with arrogance? We cannot—at least not in truth.

So what does Satan ultimately want to accomplish through his many schemes? He wants to destroy our faith in Christ, a matter we will consider in more detail in chapter 8. When Paul was anxious about the spiritual state of the new Thessalonian believers, he put it like this: "For this reason, when I could no longer endure it, I sent to know *your faith*, lest by some means the tempter had tempted you, and our labor might be in vain" (1 Thess. 3:5, emphasis added). Paul's fear was that Satan, the tempter, had so worked through the persecution the Thessalonians were experiencing that he had weakened their faith, thus making the apostle's labor among them fruitless.

Similarly, Jesus says to Peter on the night of his betrayal, "Simon, Simon! Indeed, Satan has asked for you, that he might sift you as wheat. But I have prayed for you, that *your faith* should not fail; and when you have returned to Me, strengthen your brethren" (Luke 22:31–32, emphasis added). Satan's design in Peter's denials was to separate Peter from his faith in Christ, as harvesters would separate the edible grain of wheat from the stalks and husks. Jesus' prayer was that Peter's faith would not fail. Although Peter sinned by denying his Lord, his faith was preserved through Jesus' prayers, evidenced by the disciple's repentance (Mark 14:72; Luke 22:61–62).

In addition, we read in Revelation 2:10 that Satan can try our faith by bringing persecutions upon us, "Do not fear any of those things which you are about to suffer. Indeed, the devil is about to throw some of you into prison, that you may be tested, and you will have tribulation ten days. Be faithful until death, and I will give you the crown of life."

Since Satan seeks to destroy our faith in Christ through a variety of ways, how shall we, as Christians, respond? Shall we collapse in fear? Be filled with anxiety and uncertainty? Absolutely not. Rather, we must always remember that although Satan is strong, he is not as strong as he might seem. J. I. Packer says concerning the devil, "He should be taken seriously, for malice and cunning make him fearsome; yet not so seriously as to provoke abject terror of him, for he is a beaten enemy. Satan is stronger than we are, but Christ has triumphed over Satan (Matt. 12:29), and Christians will triumph over him too if they resist him with the resources that Christ supplies (Eph. 6:10–13; James 4:7; 1 Peter 5:9–10)."[7]

Soldiers of Christ, we must stand, and one of the ways we stand is by knowing our enemy and the schemes he employs against us. We must see that he is targeting the destruction of our faith. Identify his lies through the truth of God's Word. Stand firm in that truth by faith. Christ Jesus has already won our victory. Therefore, we can stand. We can resist in the name of the One who has struck the fatal blow.

---

7. J. I. Packer, *Concise Theology* (Wheaton, Ill.: Tyndale House, 1993), 70.

FOR REFLECTION AND DISCUSSION

1. Identify and describe any schemes or tactics that Satan has successfully used against you.

2. Identify and describe any specific lies that Satan has used to bait you.

3. What specific areas of God's character has Satan challenged in your life?

4. How has your faith in Christ been weakened under these attacks? How has your faith in Christ been preserved in these attacks?

CHAPTER 4

The Nature of Our Conflict

For we do not wrestle against flesh and blood, but against principalities, against powers, against the rulers of the darkness of this age, against spiritual hosts of wickedness in the heavenly places. Therefore take up the whole armor of God, that you may be able to withstand in the evil day, and having done all, to stand.

—EPHESIANS 6:12–13

German New Testament scholar Rudolph Bultmann famously said that if you turn on an electric light, you most certainly could not believe in demons. His point was clear: living in the modern world of science and technology has forced many people to leave behind the premodern, prescientific, primitive beliefs that people generally held prior to the advent of lightbulbs. Under this kind of liberal and "intellectual" influence, it became increasingly popular for biblical scholars to assert that the fourfold "principalities," "powers," "rulers of the darkness," and "spiritual hosts of wickedness" in Ephesians 6:12 describe the evils that exist within socioeconomic political structures rather than real, demonic, spiritual enemies in the world. According to the likes of Bultmann and others, the way we need to understand the apostle Paul is that we fight against impersonal social forces and nothing more.

Paul, however, was more enlightened than Bultmann—lightbulb or no lightbulb! According to the inspired apostle, our conflict is with real, personal adversaries—namely, the devil and his cohorts, the demons. Reformed theologian Charles Hodge agreed with Paul and reminded his nineteenth-century readers that the language of Ephesians 6:10–20 is not "a figure of speech. It is something real and arduous."[1]

WARFARE REVIEW

We must not lose sight of the first principles that we have already considered. "Be strong in the Lord and in the power of His might" connects us back to the resurrected, ascended, exalted, enthroned, and victorious Jesus. In order for us to be empowered for spiritual warfare, we must constantly rely on Christ, our risen Lord. "Put on the whole armor of God" calls us to be protected fully with all that God supplies us in this battle. The purpose is so that we can "stand" and fully resist "the wiles of the devil." Now in verses 12–13 Paul further explains why all of this is so vitally important.

NOT AGAINST FLESH AND BLOOD

As the apostle gives us the rationale for putting on the whole armor of God, he begins verse 12 by stating a negative: "For we do not wrestle against flesh and blood." Here Paul presses upon us the main reason that we must make good use of God-provided armor. We must do this because of the supernatural, crafty nature of our conflict. He is not trying to scare us but rather to sober us up to the hostile battle at hand.

As Christians, we could tend to forget about this battle. The world's pleasures or worries can numb us. Perhaps we have accepted the world's mantra that things are getting better and evil is being removed and have therefore fallen under the delusion that there is no serious threat before us. We might become inactive in this fight, believing that spiritual warfare is a thing of the past. Here is where we must be especially on guard because such thinking will

---

1. Hodge, *Ephesians*, 274.

inevitably lead us into great trouble. We must never forget that our fight is real.

The word "wrestle" in the verse is key, as it defines the essence of our battle with our invisible opponents. Paul uses it figuratively to describe our struggle with evil forces. We might be surprised that he has used an athletic image in this passage rather than a military term. Wrestling was a popular sport in the Greco-Roman world, so this term would have resonated with Paul's readers. The apostle uses it to illustrate that in spiritual warfare we are in close-quarter combat, as with literal wrestling. The battle is similar to a hand-to-hand struggle; it is as close and intense as two wrestlers maneuvering against each other on a mat. Strong and strenuous effort all the way to glory is therefore required.

This image is contrary to how some popular preachers portray the Christian life; it is not always a "walk in the park." While for Christians this life is the best possible *on this side of glory*, they nonetheless have actual enemies who would love nothing more than to immobilize and defeat them. Christians are engaged in a holy war, a life-and-death spiritual battle. This war does not take place on a literal battlefield or in the streets during some popular uprising; instead, it takes place in our minds, members, and hearts.

When Paul says our struggle is not against "flesh and blood," he uses a first-century Jewish way of saying that this conflict is not with weak, frail human beings. Although people may be used as weapons in the battle (Eph. 4:14), they are not the ultimate enemy. To intensify the contrast to such a notion, Paul identifies the enemies with whom we do wrestle with a fourfold use of the word *against* in the second half of verse 12: "*against* principalities, *against* powers, *against* the rulers of the darkness of this age, *against* spiritual hosts of wickedness in the heavenly places" (emphasis added).

Some Bible teachers believe that this series of spiritual enemies is an elaborate and definitive description of the hierarchical structure of the spirit world. They see it as a catalog of four different classes of demonic beings. Peter O'Brien notes, however, "The different terms point to the same reality and any attempt to rank them is pure speculation."[2] Clinton Arnold concurs: "While the terms may imply a hierarchy within the demonic realm, we have no means of discerning the various ranks by the use of these terms."[3]

Each of the words Paul uses is instructive for our understanding of the whole range of spiritual enemies we face, along with the devil himself. The first word, "principalities," is a plural noun that suggests those who are of first importance or occupy eminent positions. It could refer to earthly principalities or rulers or spiritual ones (cf. Luke 12:11; Col. 1:16). The next word, "powers," is used with "principalities" in Ephesians 1:21 and 3:10 and connotes demonic spirits. The phrase "the rulers of the darkness of this age" is used only here in the New Testament, and it represents the menacing powers of the kingdom of Satan and the reality of their influence at this present time (cf. Col. 1:13). "Spiritual hosts of wickedness in the heavenly places" completes the list of demonic powers and shows that our warfare is definitely not on a human level. The phrase "spiritual hosts," in the original language, is simply "the spirituals," or that which belongs to the spirit world as opposed to the natural world. The "of wickedness" means "which are evil," and "in the heavenly places" tells of the dominant sphere or realm the hosts occupy.

In light of this list, we must state again that these various "behind-the-scene" powers are real. They are personal, wicked spirit beings—demons. They are not fantasy or fiction. While many people would dismiss these spirit beings as phony, we must not. God is telling us about their reality and activity for our profit and protection. In His wisdom, He knows that it is best for us to have this knowledge for our spiritual well-being.

Satan would love us to ignore these realities and simply believe that he and his associates are fake religious myths or superstitious legends. That way, he can strike when he likes, and we will never be expecting it. What trickery! Therefore, to keep secure from such

---

2. O'Brien, *Letter to the Ephesians*, 468.

3. Clinton E. Arnold, *Three Crucial Questions about Spiritual Warfare* (Grand Rapids: Baker, 1997), 39.

things, we must believe all that God has said to us in His Word and not give Satan the opportunity he seeks.

In this description, the apostle pulls back the curtain to reveal the seriousness of our warfare and gives us a glimpse of exactly whom we are up against. As William Gurnall writes in *The Christian in Complete Armour*, "Here Paul lays all on the table. He does not underrate the fierceness of the struggle or the strength of the foe. In this he is unlike Satan, who dares not let sinners know the true character of God, but must draw them on to the field with false reports and keep them there with lies and subterfuge. Paul, on the other hand, is not afraid to show the Saints their enemy in all his power."[4]

Because of the fierceness of our enemy and the true nature of our struggle, Paul exhorts his readers again to "take up the whole armor of God" (v. 13). Given that such cosmic powers are pitted against us, he essentially repeats what he called us to do in verse 11 so that we do not take his instructions lightly. To oppose evil spiritual powers, we need a power greater than our own—a power even greater than that of these spiritual foes. We need nothing less than the power of God, and He gives this to His people in the "whole armor of God."

Paul reiterates the purpose for taking up this armor: "that you may be able to withstand in the evil day" (v. 13). Here, we should understand that these words apply corporately, since in the Greek language the main verbs in the phrase are in the second person plural. Although each Christian has personal responsibility before God in this war, the use of plurals reminds us that as believers we stand together, establishing a unified resistance against the evil one.

Just as we need battle support from our brothers and sisters in the Lord in spiritual warfare, they need it from us, so we should pray for them and encourage them often. Let us inquire of them frequently, asking what battles they are facing so that we can come alongside and aid them. In this war, we are our brother's keeper. We are to have great care and concern for one another. As Roman

---

4. William Gurnall, *The Christian in Complete Armour* (Edinburgh: Banner of Truth, 1986), 1:124.

soldiers would often stand shoulder-to-shoulder and shield-to-shield for greater protection, so also we must take up God's armor and stand strong as one!

Expositors have understood the words "evil day" in verse 13 in various ways. Most likely the phrase refers either to this present evil age (Gal. 1:4; Eph. 5:16) or to a specifically severe trial in daily life (for example, in Luke 22:31). In either case, we need to understand that, as believers, we wake up and go to bed in the evil day. Not all days are equally dangerous, but the point is we can never completely rest comfortably. The assaults will likely come when we least expect them.

Paul's final exhortation is "and having done all, to stand" (v. 13). With these words, the apostle is reinforcing all that he has just said. The Christian is a man of war, and as a good soldier of the Lord Jesus Christ, he is to maintain his spiritual position throughout life. The believer lives on the spiritual battlefield and, having fully prepared for battle, he is to remain fixed in his position. In sum, he is to hold fast the solid ground that Jesus has already won for him in His life. We should take the words of Martyn Lloyd-Jones to heart:

> The Christian has put on the whole armor of God, he is filled with the strength and the power, and he has fought the battle in the evil day. Then having done all, he is tempted to take off his armor. "I have gained the victory," he says, "all is well." Then, taking off his armor, he lies down on his bed. "No," says the apostle, "having done all—stand!" Go on standing. Do not relax. "Maintain the field!" You are always on duty in the Christian life, you can never relax. There is no such thing as a holiday in the spiritual realm.[5]

May the Lord help us to remember this as we fight in this great battle.

---

5. Lloyd-Jones, *Christian Soldier*, 153.

FOR REFLECTION AND DISCUSSION

1. What is your worldview concerning spiritual realities, such as the existence of demonic spirits? Are your beliefs biblical?

2. Paul says our battle is not against flesh and blood. Describe a time when you may have forgotten this truth. What was the result?

3. What are some ways in which you can help fellow believers take up the armor of God collectively and stand together in spiritual warfare?

4. Describe a recent "evil day" in your life. Were you prepared?

CHAPTER 5

The Belt of Truth

Stand therefore, having girded your waist with truth...
—EPHESIANS 6:14

In *Our Sufficiency in Christ,* John MacArthur writes:

> I am amazed at the number of Christians being drawn into the
> burgeoning "spiritual warfare" movement. I am convinced it
> represents an unhealthy obsession with Satan and demonic
> powers. Judging from the turnouts, thousands of Christians
> really believe that if you don't attend a spiritual-warfare boot
> camp and learn some strategies for fighting demons, Satan will
> have them for breakfast. Is that true? Is there some secret strat-
> egy to be learned from "experts" in the art of spiritual warfare?
> Do Christians need to study mystic techniques for confronting
> and commanding evil forces, "binding" the devil, "breaking
> the strongholds" of territorial demons, and other complex
> stratagems of metaphysical combat? Is it simplistic to think
> that the basic armor described in Ephesians 6 is sufficient to
> keep us from being breakfast for Satan? Absolutely not.[1]

How do we stand biblically against the great enemy of our souls?
What weapons do we use in this great fight of faith? God would
not have us engage in spiritual warfare in a fruitless and futile way.
Rather, He has given us helpful instruction and a powerful arsenal
that are mighty against the devil.

---

1. John MacArthur, *Our Sufficiency in Christ* (Dallas: Word Publishing,
1991), 214–15.

In the next several chapters, we will examine this instruction in detail, considering each of the six pieces of spiritual armor that God calls us to put on. We have seen that the war for our souls has been won because of Christ's death and resurrection for us, and that, in union with Him, we have His resurrection power available for spiritual warfare. We will now consider the practical matter of what it means to take up the whole armor of God so that we can stand effectively as soldiers in the Lord's army.

In Ephesians 6:14–17 the apostle Paul sketches a picture of the spiritual resources that are ours for this conflict. We believe that Paul's imagery here reflects the concept of God as the well-armored, divine warrior-king of His people, as discussed in chapter 2. It also seems that while Paul was sitting in prison in Rome, the Holy Spirit moved him to consider the armor of the Roman soldiers around him, and he drew from that situation spiritual lessons for how we can engage in the battle that we must face as Christians.

PREPARE FOR BATTLE

The apostle begins verse 14 by commanding us to "stand" for the fourth time in this section.[2] So struck is Paul with the seriousness of the subject and our doing well that he implores us again to stand and not surrender. Paul does not want us to lose any spiritual ground in our lives. Satan loves nothing more than to see God's people regress. He loves to see believers stunted and stumbling on their way to heaven. The apostle would not have this. He would have us to progress in the things of God from strength to strength; therefore, he calls us to be perpetually alert, always prepared to ward off the advances of our spiritual opponent with unyielding defense. As Stanley Gale says:

---

2. Peter T. O'Brien says, "The four participles which follow the imperative 'stand' namely, 'having fastened the belt of truth,' 'having put on the breastplate of righteousness' (v. 14), 'having fitted your feet' (v. 15), and 'having taken up the shield of faith' (v. 16), spell out the actions believers need to have taken if they are to stand firm." Letter to the Ephesians, 473.

Spiritual armor is the uniform of the day. We want to live in a state of alertness and readiness, recognizing that sin crouches at our door and its desire is for us. Our enemy the devil prowls about like a roaring lion seeking to devour, opposing us in Christian life and service. So we live, on the one hand, at peace because Christ has overcome the world (John 16:33). Yet, on the other, we live on the edge, and on guard, cognizant of our spiritual enemy yet confident in the victory of our Savior.[3]

Paul adds that we are to stand, "having girded [our] waist with truth." The image here is of a belt, and the apostle tells us that we are to have it "girded," or fastened, upon us, which means to wrap it around as preparation for activity. The idea literally means to bind it to ourselves. Several writers note that Paul derives this picture from the soldiers' custom of shortening the long, flowing tunics they wore as their primary clothing and outer garment. Ordinarily the tunic draped loosely over the soldier's body; however, when the soldier was preparing for battle, he would tuck the ends of his robe into his belt. He did this for freedom of movement so that his lengthy robe would not hinder his progress when he met the enemy. With the belt tied tightly around his waist and his garment tucked in, granting him free motion of his legs, the warrior was ready for combat. The belt was also where his sword was sheathed, which gave the warrior central support for his entire body.

Clearly, the apostle uses this imagery to call Christians to stand ready for the fight. His words signify a transition from a relaxed to an action mode.[4] In other words, the apostle is calling us to spiritual arms. War is upon us. The alarm has sounded. The battle lines have been drawn; therefore, we must responsibly gird ourselves for holy, active combat. Paul hands us our first piece of equipment, and we must put it on to be ready.

---

3. Gale, *What Is Spiritual Warfare?*, 25.
4. This idea comes from a sermon on this verse by Pastor Andy Dunkerton of the Grace Reformed Baptist Church of Mebane, North Carolina.

THE WHOLE TRUTH AND NOTHING BUT THE TRUTH

The truth is our first line of spiritual defense against the devil. Truth is an indispensable piece of armor; it functions spiritually as the believer's belt. We can imagine Paul the prisoner glancing over at his guard as he wrote this letter. Undoubtedly, he noticed the thick leather belt around the soldier's waist, the central piece of equipment he wore. So the apostle begins his list of spiritual armor by writing metaphorically about the belt that we are to wear: *As the soldier's belt was placed at the center of his body, so truth must be central in our lives, encompassing all that we do if we are to be prepared for the fight with Satan, our crafty foe.*

By truth we bind up everything in our lives that is loose that might cause us to stumble in spiritual battle. Without truth girded about us, we will stumble and be overtaken. Keeping with the metaphor, even today a belt remains an essential piece of clothing. Our belts keep the things we wear in their proper place. Further, in various professions and trades, a belt is essential to being properly equipped for the job. What hangs from a police officer's or construction worker's belt? All the necessary tools of the trade, which must be easily accessed, reside there. It is really no surprise, then, that Paul begins his illustration with such a vital piece of equipment. It is strategic in the spiritual sense because without it, nothing else will stay in place. Without the belt of truth, we are exposed and utterly vulnerable to the devil's schemes and are unable to stand against him.

It is also important for us to consider something of the nature of the belt of truth. Some have wondered whether the truth that Paul mentions in this passage is the objective theological truth concerning God, Christ, and the gospel (1:13; 4:21), or if it refers to the more subjective aspect of living according to truth as believers (4:15, 25; 5:9). Given Paul's use of the noun *truth* in this letter, why must we choose between these two? The apostle uses the word *truth* in both senses throughout this epistle. Further, the two concepts certainly go together. The belt of truth, then, refers to the truths of God as contained in His Word and our living uprightly because we have been saved by those truths.

Concerning this matter, Harold Hoehner writes in his commentary on Ephesians:

> Believers have girded their waist with God's objective truth, which in turn has become part of them. This enables them to be reliable and faithful as God is reliable and faithful. This piece of armor is basic to all other pieces because truth and trustworthiness are basic to all the qualities that believers need in order to withstand diabolical attacks. As believers internalize God's truth they live and move in it.[5]

We see, then, the vital importance of savingly embracing the truths of the gospel and consistently cultivating a true expression of the gospel life. If we neglect either of these, we leave ourselves open to be "tossed to and fro and carried about with every wind of doctrine" (4:14). Since God's Word is truth (John 17:17), and we have been saved by Jesus who is the truth (John 14:6), we are to walk in truth (3 John 1:3–4) so that we will not be tricked by the enemy or his emissaries,[6] who love to twist the truth (Gen. 3:1; Matt. 7:15; Acts 20:28–30).

This twofold understanding of the belt of truth gives us the full picture of what we are spiritually to wrap around ourselves daily. First, understanding the belt of truth *objectively* means that daily we must be studying the Word of God and submitting to its truth. Regularly we must be meditating and memorizing its contents so that we will be strengthened in the inner man against the lies, deceits, and errors of the adversary. God's divine truth as contained in the Bible is the great antidote to falsehood. As Christians, we are called to let the word of Christ dwell richly within us (Col. 3:16) and to

---

5. Harold Hoehner, *Ephesians: An Exegetical Commentary* (Grand Rapids: Baker Academic, 2002), 839–40.

6. For a very helpful treatment on resisting false teachers, see "Seven Characteristics of False Teachers," in *Precious Remedies against Satan's Devices*, by Thomas Brooks (Edinburgh: Banner of Truth, 1984), 230. Also, for a detailed exposition of Matthew 7:15–20, which speaks against false teachers, listen to the sermon "Jesus' Warnings against False Teachers," by Rob Ventura, at www.sermonaudio.com/sermoninfo.asp?SID=41711152187.

hide God's Word in our heart (Ps. 119:11) so that it will spiritually support us as a belt supports the waist.

Too often believers fail at this point. They seek to stand against the wiles of the devil with their own native resources and *without* the spiritual nutrients of Scripture. When they do this, they are no match for the devil. Lloyd-Jones comments, "You must gird yourselves and your loins with truth. If you do not, you are defeated. And I am asserting and maintaining that truth can be known, that there is an authority. It is not reason, it is not feelings, it is not the Church, any church. It is the book called the Bible."[7]

Believer, are you persuaded that if you are to stand strong against the schemes of the devil in your life, you must be a person of the Book? Do you understand that your enemy is an evil foe and only the truths of the Bible will keep him in check in your life? Without God's truths at the center of your being—in your heart and mind—you are bound to fail. The devil is a master at his craft, and he has perfected his diabolical methods against us. He has slain his thousands; however, with the Word of God in you and part of you, you will be able to stand victoriously against his temptations and traps. This is why the apostle John could say, "I have written to you…because you are strong, and the word of God abides in you, and you have overcome the wicked one" (1 John 2:14).

As Christians, we are to delight ourselves in the Scriptures, saying with the psalmist, "Oh, how I love your law! It is my meditation all the day" (Ps. 119:97). When the storms of Satan are upon us, we must completely trust in all that God's Word says, remembering that no weapon formed against us shall prosper (Isa. 54:17).

Second, understanding the belt of truth *subjectively* means that by the power of the Holy Spirit and the grace of God we are to live out the demands of the gospel by "denying ungodliness and worldly lusts," and conduct ourselves "soberly, righteously, and godly in the present age" (Titus 2:12). If we are not personally and persistently walking in the truths of God in every area of life "in the inward

---

7. Lloyd-Jones, *Christian Soldier*, 206.

parts" (Ps. 51:6), we are leaving ourselves open to all kinds of spiritual trouble because we are playing into the hand of our enemy, who would love to see our demise. Remember, Satan is a deceiver (Rev. 12:9). He is the devil, the father of lies (John 8:44). Therefore, if we entertain *un*truth and *un*righteousness at any point, we give him opportunity to harm us greatly. Paul warns us never to give the devil this opportunity, pointing out specifically the dangers of lying and being angry: "Putting away lying, 'Let each one of you speak truth with his neighbor,' for we are members of one another. 'Be angry, and do not sin': do not let the sun go down on your wrath, *nor give place to the devil*" (Eph. 4:25–27, emphasis added).

If we are not walking in the truth—being governed and possessed by it—if we are living hypocritically, then we are incapacitating ourselves for spiritual combat and will be defeated. We are essentially inviting the enemy of our souls to come have his way with us, having weakened ourselves through sin. Why would we ever put ourselves in such danger? Do we care so little for our soul's well-being? May it never be!

You must be on guard. Personal sin will cause you to stumble, dishonor God, and lose great blessings in your life. The devil will use your sin to make you miserable and ineffectual. The backslidden King David demonstrates that personal sin is a great albatross around our necks (Ps. 32:3–4), so flee from it to Jesus, knowing that He always gives aid to all who come to Him for help (Heb. 2:16–18; 4:14–16). If you are not living a holy life by mortifying sin by the power of the Spirit (Rom. 8:13) and by walking in the ways of God's truth by His grace, you will be weighed down with guilt and, like a soldier trying to run through a battlefield with his robe around his ankles, you will fall.[8] Warren Wiersbe observes, "Unless we are motivated and directed by truth, we will be defeated by the enemy. If we permit any deception to enter our lives, we have weakened our position and cannot fight the battle victoriously. The girdle of truth

---

8. This illustration comes from *The Purpose of God: An Exposition of Ephesians*, by R. C. Sproul (Fearn, Ross-shire, Scotland: Christian Focus, 1994), 148.

is not an offensive weapon; it is for protection. When the believer has what I call 'an attitude of truth' in his life, this protects him from Satan's attacks."[9]

We need to examine ourselves. Do you have "an attitude of truth"? Are you embracing God's Word in the inner man, allowing it to direct your life? If so, rejoice! However, insofar as we find ourselves falling short, let us go to Christ, who loves to forgive and renew all who come to Him by faith (John 6:37; 1 John 1:7–10).

FOR REFLECTION AND DISCUSSION

1. Explain why the spiritual battle you are in has a serious nature. What is at stake for you if you do not put on the belt of truth?

2. What are some areas of your life where truth is eroding? How will you bring God's truth to these areas?

3. If you do not bring truth to these areas, what will be the nature of your defeat? Write down biblical, historical, or personal examples where defeat resulted from inattention to living truthfully.

4. How is it that you can better learn the objective truths of God and the gospel for your own life so that you can stand strong against the devil?

---

9. Warren W. Wiersbe, *The Strategy of Satan: How to Detect and Defeat Him* (Wheaton, Ill.: Tyndale, 1979), 129.

CHAPTER 6

The Breastplate of Righteousness

...having put on the breastplate of righteousness...
—EPHESIANS 6:14

Having unveiled the first, most fundamental piece of spiritual equipment, the belt of truth, Paul now reveals the second, the breastplate of righteousness. The apostle has already commanded us to stand, but he knows that we can do so only if we wear this next essential protective layer. Paul uses the Greek word for "put on" in this verse metaphorically for the last time in this letter.

We must not overlook the sense of these words. He is teaching us that when it comes to the armor of God, we are not merely to admire the various pieces or put them in some fancy display case; rather, we are to use them. The only way we can stand in this spiritual fight is by actually using what God has given us for the battle, and we must be persuaded of this as well. Too often believers mistakenly think that they can coast in the Christian life or use means that are not biblical to achieve success. Here again Paul places the responsibility on us. Since we are in a real spiritual battle, it is only as we put on and employ all the spiritual armor that we will be successful.

BE PROTECTED

In Paul's day, the soldier's breastplate was a layer of metal or very tough leather that covered the soldier from his neck to his navel, both front and back. The breastplate provided crucial protection from mortal wounds. This description informs our understanding of our spiritual warfare. *The breastplate was a chief piece of defensive armor for a soldier because it protected his vital organs during battle, and it serves the same function for us spiritually in our battle with Satan.* As inconceivable as it is that a soldier would go to war without protecting his vital organs, it should be even more inconceivable for us that we would enter into warfare with the devil without protecting ourselves. Spiritually speaking, this breastplate covers one of the main areas the devil seeks to attack most often—our hearts. Joel Beeke comments: "People in Paul's day believed that organs such as the heart and the liver were the center of affections. Emotions, such as joy or anger, originated in these organs. The apostle Paul used this understanding, unscientific though it was, to teach important spiritual lessons. He said believers must put on the breastplate of righteousness to protect the vital parts of the inner man and its faculties against the attacks of Satan."[1]

Proverbs 4:23 tells us that believers must protect their hearts because from them "spring the issues of life." In other words, everything we say, think, or do flows from our hearts. Often in Scripture, the heart represents all that we are, the whole inner person. Texts such as Deuteronomy 30:1–3; Hosea 10:2; Matthew 22:37; Luke 12:34; and Luke 21:34 point this out. The heart is where we reason and make decisions; it is where our values reside. It is where our intentions, motivations, opinions, and judgments are formed. Jerry Bridges explains what *heart* means:

> *Heart* in Scripture is used in various ways. Sometimes it means our reason or understanding, sometimes our affections and emotion, and sometimes our will. Generally it denotes the whole soul of man and all its faculties, not individually, but as they all work together in doing good or evil. The mind as it reasons, discerns, and judges; the emotions as they like or dislike; the conscience as it determines and warns; and the will as it chooses or refuses—are all together called the heart.[2]

---

1. Joel Beeke, *Striving against Satan* (Wales: Bryntirion, 2006), 46.
2. Jerry Bridges, *The Pursuit of Holiness* (Colorado Springs: NavPress, 1978), 63–64.

Since all that we are resides within our hearts, it is plain to see why Paul calls us to protect them spiritually. If we leave our hearts exposed to the enemy's attacks, we can be fatally wounded. If the devil, with all his deceptions and pernicious ways, can penetrate us deep within, then he can put us into a most deplorable spiritual condition. If the enemy's subtle suggestions penetrate our hearts, they can cause us great ruin. If the devil's attacks reach the core of our being, he can influence us to live with guilt, fear, anxiety, depression,[3] and discouragement. We must not allow him to do this. Satan knows where we are most vulnerable. Therefore, we ought to heed Paul's admonition seriously.

OUR IMPENETRABLE COVERING

There are two main views concerning the meaning of *righteousness* in this passage. Some say that Paul is referring to the *objective righteousness* of Christ that God imputes to the believer (Rom. 4:6–11; 2 Cor. 5:21; Phil. 3:9). This view seems convincing because Christ's perfect, unassailable righteousness is a predominant theme in Paul's writings. No matter how hot the battle, our imputed righteousness—because it is Christ's—cannot be, in any way, diminished or jeopardized. Our standing before God is completely secure once for all through Christ's covering, and no attack of Satan can change this. Our hearts, then, are thoroughly protected from Satan's accusations and lies, that we might withstand them.

This first interpretation of *righteousness* calls us continually to remember the flawless righteousness of our Lord when the devil brings a railing accusation against us. Our adversary accuses us saying, "What? You sinned again? That is because you are no good. Look how often you sin! You are nothing but a hypocrite. God wants

---

3. Some helpful resources on spiritual depression that address the matter of demonic activity include *Spiritual Depression: Its Causes and Cure*, by D. Martyn Lloyd-Jones (Grand Rapids: Eerdmans, 1965); *Christians Get Depressed Too*, by David Murray (Grand Rapids: Reformation Heritage Books, 2010); and *Overcoming Spiritual Depression*, by Arie Elshout (Grand Rapids: Reformation Heritage Books, 2006).

nothing to do with hypocrites." The devil rubs our faces in our failures. He seeks to paralyze us and rob us of our joy and delight in the Lord. What are we to do in response to this? Certainly, we cannot proclaim our *own* righteousness to him since it is nothing more than filthy rags (Isa. 64:6). Rather, we should promptly confess our sins to God. We must assure ourselves that although we are full of remaining sin, nonetheless, according to Romans 8:1, "there is therefore now no condemnation to those who are in Christ Jesus." When the devil points his accusing finger at us, we should say with the apostle Paul, "Who shall bring a charge against God's elect? It is God who justifies. Who is he who condemns? It is Christ who died, and furthermore is also risen, who is even at the right hand of God, who also makes intercession for us" (Rom. 8:33–34).

What great confidence, then, the objective righteousness of Christ gives to the true believer! It is the anchor of the soul when the devil comes against us. Our identity is in Christ, and Christ's righteousness has been legally credited to our account in the courtroom of heaven. Therefore, when the slanderer comes against us, we must stand firm and say with the hymn writer,

> Jesus, Thy blood and righteousness
> My beauty are, my glorious dress;
> 'Midst flaming worlds, in these arrayed,
> With joy shall I lift up my head.

> Bold shall I stand in Thy great day;
> For who aught to my charge shall lay?
> Fully absolved through these I am
> From sin and fear, from guilt and shame.[4]

Concerning this objective righteousness of Christ, John Eadie writes,

> When the justifying righteousness of Christ is assumed as a breastplate by sinners, they can defy the assaults of the tempter. To every insinuation that they are so vile, guilty, worthless and perverse—so beset with sin and under such wrath that God

---

4. Nikolaus L. von Zinzendorf, "Jesus, Thy Blood and Righteousness."

will repulse them—they oppose the free and perfect righteousness of their Redeemer, which is "upon them" (Rom. 3:22). So that the dart thrown at them only rings against such a cuirass [breastplate], and falls blunted to the earth.[5]

The second major view is that Paul is writing of a *subjective righteousness* that is to characterize the Christian's daily experience, which has also been called an ethical, or practical, righteousness. The Puritans distinguished this righteousness from the imputed righteousness of Christ by calling it the imparted righteousness of the believer.

This understanding of the breastplate of righteousness is also convincing because it fits nicely into the overall thrust of this letter. Twice in Ephesians Paul has called this church to practical, godly living (4:24–25; 5:8–9) and reminded them that they are to be holy because God chose them (1:4). Elsewhere, Paul writes that the substance of the breastplate is "faith and love," both of which fall under the sphere of subjective righteousness (1 Thess. 5:8).

When we understand the breastplate of righteousness as subjective, we see that we must live uprightly with a good conscience in all areas of life (Acts 24:16; 2 Cor. 1:12), and, as we do, our hearts will be protected and fortified when the devil seeks to lure us to sin. We will not want to follow him. Lehman Strauss says in his commentary on Ephesians:

> The righteous ones are the redeemed ones, and to all such God says: "yield yourselves unto God, as those that are alive from the dead, and your members as instruments of righteousness unto God" (Rom. 6:13). If we are not living righteously we are easy targets for the enemy's darts. Sinning saints cannot stand in the day of adversity when Satan attacks. Right living is wound-proof; therefore, "we should live soberly, righteously, and godly, in this present world" (Titus 2:12).[6]

---

5. John Eadie, *A Commentary on the Greek Text of Paul's Letter to the Ephesians* (Birmingham, Ala.: Solid Ground Christian Books, 2005), 468.

6. Lehman Strauss, *Devotional Studies in Galatians and Ephesians* (New York: Loizeaux Brothers, 1957), 230.

So how are we to understand the word *righteousness* in this passage: Christ's imputed righteousness given to the believing sinner, or the believer's daily upright living that resists Satan's solicitations to evil? Both meanings are indicated here because a believer cannot have imparted righteousness without first having the imputed righteousness of Christ, and a person who has the imputed righteousness of Christ must live a life that reflects the will of Christ. Biblical purity and holiness of character are the fruits of someone who is saved. Subjective righteousness has its roots in objective righteousness; the two belong together in an integrated whole.[7] Clinton Arnold offers this biblically balanced observation: "Some scholars limit the understanding of breastplate of righteousness to this objective gift of God's justifying righteousness, but in light of Paul's earlier statements in this letter about the pursuit of righteousness, it also indicates the importance of cultivating righteous living.... Possessing God's righteousness necessarily leads to a life of holiness."[8]

As believers, we completely and solely rest in our acceptance before God because of Christ's work alone on our behalf. Jesus is "THE LORD OUR RIGHTEOUSNESS" (Jer. 23:6). His perfect merits are ours by faith alone apart from our works (Rom. 4:1–6). His life, death, and resurrection are the complete and final grounds of our acceptance before the Father. We are accepted in the Beloved (Eph. 1:6). When God looks at us, He does not see our filth and sin; rather, He sees the beauties and perfections of His Son that have been credited to our account. As Christians, our standing before the Almighty is not *only* "just-as-if-we-never-sinned." Because of Christ's righteousness, which God has reckoned to us, it is "just-as-if-we-lived-a-perfect-life."[9]

What great hope, joy, and confidence this should bring us! When John Bunyan was saved, he greatly rejoiced in this righteousness of

---

7. Sinclair B. Ferguson, *Let's Study Ephesians* (Edinburgh: Banner of Truth, 2005), 181.

8. Arnold, *Exegetical Commentary on the New Testament,* 453.

9. Wayne Grudem, *Systematic Theology* (Grand Rapids: Zondervan, 1994), 727.

Christ, and he writes about this in his autobiography, *Grace Abounding to the Chief of Sinners*:

> One day, as I was passing in the field, and that too with some dashes of my conscience, fearing lest yet all was not right, suddenly this sentence fell upon my soul, Thy righteousness is in heaven; and methought withal, I saw, with the eyes of my soul, Jesus Christ at God's right hand; there, I say, as my righteousness; so that wherever I was, or whatever I was adoing, God could not say of me, He wants my righteousness, for that was just before Him. I also saw, moreover, that it was not my good frame of heart that made my righteousness better, nor yet my bad frame that made my righteousness worse; for my righteousness was Jesus Christ Himself, the same yesterday, to-day and for ever. Now did my chains fall off my legs indeed, I was loosened from my afflictions and irons.... Now went I also home rejoicing, for the grace and love of God.[10]

Nonetheless, because Jesus has saved us, the Spirit enables us to walk continually on the straight and narrow path that leads to life. Now that we are saved, we have the Holy Spirit within us who causes us to walk in God's statutes and keep His decrees (Ezek. 36:27). We are dead indeed to sin and alive to God in Christ Jesus our Lord; therefore, we are not to let sin reign in our mortal body to make us obey its passions (Rom. 6:11–12). We are no longer slaves to sin but slaves to righteousness (Rom. 6:17–18). With this reality before us, we must live accordingly.

If we toy with sin in our lives, we leave ourselves open to be wounded in battle like Ahab, who was struck "between the scale armor and the breastplate" (1 Kings 22:34 ESV). However, if we walk in the light as God is in the light, the devil will gain no foothold with us. Believer, this places a great duty on you. You must not live passively. You must engage all of your redeemed faculties to live in a way that pleases God. Whereas "salvation is of the LORD"

---

10. John Bunyan, *Grace Abounding to the Chief of Sinners*, in *The Works of John Bunyan*, ed. George Offor (1854; repr., Edinburgh: Banner of Truth, 1991), 35–36.

(Jonah 2:9), sanctification is your working with God, who works in you "both to will and to do for His good pleasure" (Phil. 2:12–13).

In light of all of this, do you see how vital it is for you to "stand… having put on the breastplate of righteousness"? The breastplate of righteousness is a key safeguard for you. Never take it off. Daily meditate on Christ's perfections, which are yours before God, and daily seek to live a holy life—being "blameless and harmless, children of God without fault in the midst of a crooked and perverse generation, among whom you shine as lights in the world" (Phil. 2:15).

In summary, Paul says in Ephesians 6:14 that for us to stand strong against the assaults of the devil, we need both aspects of the breastplate of righteousness covering our hearts: legal and ethical. This is our spiritual breastplate. If we are not constantly mindful of our righteous standing in Christ or if we are not striving to live righteous lives by God's grace, we become easy targets for the adversary. May God help us, then, in both of these aspects.

A WORD TO THE READER

We would not be so naive to think that everyone who reads this book is a true Christian, and so we ask you this: Do you have the righteousness of Jesus Christ imputed to your account? Have you been saved by grace alone, through faith alone, in Christ alone, with the evidence of that salvation being a transformed life (2 Cor. 5:17)? Have you turned from your sins and asked Jesus to forgive you all your trespasses against God based on His work on the cross in the place of sinners? Jesus died, the just for the unjust, that He might bring us to God. On the cross, He paid the debt sinners owed to God by bearing the full weight of His judgment due them upon Himself. Therefore, we urge you, if you have not done so, turn from your sins and trust exclusively in Christ and His finished work on the cross of Calvary.

FOR REFLECTION AND DISCUSSION

1. Why is it important to protect your mind and emotions?

2. How does the objective sense of the breastplate of righteousness (imputed righteousness) specifically comfort and protect your heart and mind?

3. How does ethical righteousness protect your heart and mind? Caution: be on guard against answering this question in a way that promotes self-righteousness or works-righteousness.

4. Explain why Christ's righteousness gives you more comfort and protection than your ethical righteousness.

CHAPTER 7

The Gospel of Peace Footwear

*…having shod your feet with the preparation of the
gospel of peace…*
— EPHESIANS 6:15

In this chapter, we take up our third piece of spiritual armor, which,
like all the others, we must understand and apply in a biblical and
balanced way so that we have an accurate understanding of spiritual
warfare. Thus far, Paul has charged us to protect our waists and our
hearts. Now we are called to "stand…having shod [firmly fastened]
your feet with the preparation of the gospel of peace" (Eph. 6:14–15).
Shoes are very important. Whether we wear something comfortable
for our regular activities or specialized shoes for performing well in
athletics, proper footwear makes a considerable difference. As it is for
us, so it was for the warriors of old. Along with belt and breastplate,
proper footgear was a vital piece of equipment for a first-century
Roman soldier. Often involved in close-range combat, he needed to
be sure-footed since losing his balance due to inadequate footwear
could hasten his demise in battle. To fight well, he needed to move
quickly and decisively and therefore required solid footing.

Scholars tell us that the Roman soldier wore shoes that were
leather half-boots or sandals tied with straps at the ankles and
shins. The soles were thick leather, having hollow-headed hobnails
under them that greatly improved the warrior's balance.[1] These
were like the athletic cleats football and baseball players wear in our

---

1. Hoehner, *Ephesians*, 842.

day, providing the fighters a firm connection to the ground and an enhanced stability wherever they turned. Without such footgear, a soldier would never be ready for combat. He would never be able to withstand the attack of the opponent.

Paul tells us that as spiritual soldiers in Jesus' army, we are to have properly equipped feet. Specifically, he says that we are to "put on the preparation of the gospel of peace."

GOING ON THE OFFENSIVE

The term *preparation* in this verse is translated from a Greek word that appears only here in the New Testament and literally means "preparedness." It suggests the idea of promptness or readiness. So why does Paul tell us that we must have our feet prepared with the gospel of peace? There are at least two reasons. First, as believers we must always be ready to go on the offensive by taking the gospel of Jesus Christ to a lost world so that people might be saved and delivered from Satan's tyranny. If we understand *preparation* in this sense, we are to have a "readiness *to proclaim* the gospel of peace." Such texts as Romans 1:15–16 suggest this: "So, as much as is in me, I am ready to preach the gospel to you who are in Rome also. For I am not ashamed of the gospel of Christ, for it is the power of God to salvation for everyone who believes, for the Jew first and also for the Greek." Romans 10:15, in which Paul alludes to Isaiah 52:7, also supports this idea: "And how shall they preach unless they are sent? As it is written: 'How beautiful are the feet of those who preach the gospel of peace, who bring glad tidings of good things!'"

Paul clearly draws his imagery in Ephesians 6:15 from Isaiah 52:7 and emphasizes preaching the gospel. The parallels between these two texts are striking. Both speak about feet, the proclamation of good news, and peace. The Isaiah text pictures the Jewish people returning from captivity. As the exiles joyfully traveled over the hills to Zion, they were preceded by heralds who excitedly proclaimed to the watchman that remained in the Holy City, "Your God reigns!" Finally, after many years in banishment, the decree went forth telling the people they could be released from bondage and return home, and so this grand proclamation of good news went forth.

Thus, Isaiah 52:7 clarifies Paul's meaning in Ephesians. The apostle is calling believers to strap the good news of the gospel of peace to their feet. That is, as the Old Testament herald announced good news and liberation to those in bondage, God's people today must do the same, which means going forth into enemy quarters shod with the combat boots of the good news of Jesus Christ our Lord. Wherever we go and at every opportunity God grants, we must seek to assault Satan's kingdom, telling men and women who are under his power (Eph. 2:2) that spiritual freedom is found in Jesus.

Unsaved men and women are at enmity with God and are rebels against Him. But the gospel reveals God's terms of peace to them. The gospel is the good news that God sent Christ into the world to die for their sins so that they could be forgiven. By willingly taking upon Himself our sins and suffering punishment in our place on the cross, Jesus secured full pardon with God for all who repent of and turn from their sins and truly believe on Him. Jesus has also risen from the dead, so he is a living Savior for all who call upon His name in truth. As we preach this message, the Holy Spirit spiritually sets people free from Satan's captivity. Through the gospel, Jesus liberates men and women from satanic oppression and makes them children of God.

STANDING DEFENSIVELY

Second, our feet must be prepared with the gospel of peace so that we will always be ready to stand defensively against the devil by being firmly rooted in the truths of the gospel that pertain to us. The sense here is that the objective realities of the gospel, which we have experienced in our lives, are to guard our souls and keep us secure against the attacks of the evil one. When we understand *preparation* in this way, we see it as a "readiness which *comes from* the gospel of peace."

Satan is the accuser of the brethren (Rev. 12:10) and is relentless in his attacks on us. He lives to make our lives miserable. How do we stand against such a fearsome foe? The answer is the gospel of peace.

Just as the gospel is a powerful means for advancing God's truth and delivering many from Satan's clutches, it is also a powerful means for stabilizing us as believers, helping us to stand against his attacks. The gospel of peace, like the shoes of the Roman soldier, gives us firm footing in life and the ability to stand in this spiritual war.

Believers are frequently under fire from the devil. Therefore, as followers of Jesus, we need peace when the spiritual bombs of the enemy are exploding around us, when the bullets are flying by our heads—when danger seems imminent. We find that peace in the gospel. Paul says that the gospel of peace, or the gospel that has peace as its content, is that which greatly settles us in the heat of spiritual conflict.

It works practically like this: When the devil seeks to plague our consciences with guilt after we have confessed sin, we remember what the gospel of peace tells us: "If we confess our sins, He is faithful and just to forgive us our sins and to cleanse us from all unrighteousness" (1 John 1:9). When the devil condemns us, we are to bring to mind and soak our hearts deep in the comprehensive truths of the gospel and remember that God has no dispute with us because of Christ (Rom. 8:33). When the devil attacks our assurance, we must remember that we are in an unbreakable union with the living God through Jesus and that nothing will be able to "separate us from the love of God which is in Christ Jesus our Lord" (Rom. 8:39). When the devil tempts us to sin, we must push back and resist his enticements, recalling our deliverance from such things and our newness in Jesus (2 Cor. 5:17).

As Christians, we must live day-by-day in the gospel. That is, we must let its truth regularly pervade and control the citadel of our souls. God's great grace and love for us in Jesus must be our firm foundation throughout our entire lives. Here is how we will have joy, victory, and comfort despite our hardships and trials. Here is how we will be able to say with the hymn writer in the difficult day, "It is well with my soul!"

Believers sometimes think they can get beyond the gospel to "deeper things," but in truth, nothing is deeper than the gospel. The gospel is inexhaustible. It teaches us about the following:

- election, which is God's choosing of us before the foundation of the world (Eph. 1:4);

- His effectual calling, or the work of the Spirit in bringing us to Christ (2 Tim. 1:8–9);

- His propitiation, or His wrath against us appeased, through Jesus (Rom. 3:25);

- our justification, giving us acceptance before Him through faith alone in Christ alone (Rom. 5:1);

- our adoption as sons, making us part of His family (Gal. 4:5–6);

- sanctification, or His progressive work in us making us more holy (1 Thess. 5:23);

- our glorification, the final step in our redemption (1 Cor. 15:50–55).[2]

These grand themes should fill our minds constantly. We could contemplate these matters for a thousand lifetimes, if it were possible, and we would still be unable to scratch the surface!

Nonetheless, the devil loves to move us away from these glorious realities. When he does this, we are on slippery ground. However, as we meditate upon these gospel truths, when the enemy strikes we will stand strong and not fall, knowing that peace of God which surpasses all understanding, guarding our hearts and minds through Christ Jesus (Phil. 4:7). As we understand and appropriate the gospel more and more in our lives, we will advance in our ability to hold our ground when the enemy strikes.

As Roman soldiers could stand strong in the day of battle because of their specialized battle shoes, so also can the Christian when he securely wears his spiritual gospel shoes. Under enemy attack, we can dig firmly into the soil of the good news. The gospel is an indispensable part of our spiritual military equipment. It makes us immovable in the day of trouble.

---

2. For a fuller treatment of this subject, see *Redemption Accomplished and Applied*, by John Murray (Grand Rapids: Eerdmans, 1955).

FOR REFLECTION AND DISCUSSION

1. In your own words, explain why Paul tells us that we must have our feet prepared with the gospel of peace.

2. In what ways have you been involved in advancing God's gospel as a soldier in His army? How could you do this more?

3. Where in your life has the enemy scored repeated hits? What Scriptures can you bring to bear in this battle? What aspects of the gospel do you need to believe more firmly and rehearse to yourself during and after these attacks? How often have you rehearsed the gospel to yourself?

4. Are you prepared to do battle in spiritual warfare both offensively and defensively? What will you do today to prepare yourself better so that you will be ready at a moment's notice to engage? How will you make this a regular practice to increase your readiness?

CHAPTER 8

The Shield of Faith

...above all, taking the shield of faith with which
you will be able to quench all the fiery darts of the
wicked one.
— EPHESIANS 6:16

On October 27, 1861, C. H. Spurgeon preached a sermon on the shield of faith from Ephesians 6:16. He introduced his text with these words: "Like the Spartans, every Christian is born a warrior. It is his destiny to be assaulted; it is his duty to attack. Part of his life will be occupied with defensive warfare. He will have to defend earnestly the faith once delivered to the saints, he will have to resist the devil, he will have to stand against all his wiles; and having done all, still to stand."[1]

If we are to be fully equipped warriors of Christ, we need more spiritual armor, including this fourth indispensable piece. The apostle seems to draw his imagery for the shield of faith from the shield the Roman infantry used for protection in battle. Unlike the lightweight, small, round buckler shield the cavalrymen carried, this large, heavy, rectangular shield covered the warrior's entire body. Scholars tell us that this fireproof,[2] metal-lined shield was "door like," measuring around four to six feet in length and two to three feet in width. A soldier crouching behind it in battle would be completely

---

1. Charles H. Spurgeon, *Faith in All Its Splendor* (Mulberry, Ind.: Sovereign Grace Publishers, 2007), 59.

2. Several writers note that these wooden shields, covered in animal skins, were often soaked in water to extinguish burning arrows as they struck.

protected from flaming arrows. Calling forth this imagery, Paul compares faith to a protective shield. *As the shield protected a soldier in combat, so also faith spiritually protects us in every situation from whatever the devil might launch at us.*

Faith is one of the most important words in the Bible and certainly one of the richest words in Paul's vocabulary. Faith gives us victory to "overcome the world" (1 John 5:4) and is at the center of all our other spiritual defenses, encompassing all we do in spiritual battle. It is a grace that "preserves all the other graces."[3] But what kind of faith does the apostle have in view here? Is it faith in the subjective sense? In other words, is it our personal belief in God and His truth that acts as a shield? Or is it faith in the objective sense? Is it what we believe—namely, the faith once for all delivered to the saints (Jude 3), God's body of divine truth as set forth in the Bible? *Faith*, in this context, has a twofold meaning. The faith that is our shield is both subjective and objective because the subjective faith, which protects us, always involves objective faith. If our faith is to shield us, it must believe in what truly defends. Here, the two senses of the word go together (see also Eph. 1:13).

FAITH DEFINED

What does it mean for us to have faith in God and His Word? Is faith merely intellectual assent in some abstract ideas concerning God and His truth? Is it just having some vague notions or feelings about the Almighty and the Bible? It is not. Besides being the channel through which God brings us salvation (Eph. 2:8–9), faith is also what sustains us throughout the entirety of our Christian lives, for "the just *shall live* by faith" (Rom. 1:17, emphasis added). *Faith*, simply defined, is a conviction of a known truth and the solid confidence that springs from that conviction.[4] Faith is a firm persuasion

---

3. Gurnall, *Christian in Complete Armour*, 3:30.

4. John Murray has a helpful discussion of the nature of faith in *Redemption Accomplished and Applied*, 110–13. As he begins his discussion, he says, "There are three things that need to be said about the nature of faith. Faith is *knowledge, conviction and trust.*"

of and unwavering trust in God and His Son, Jesus Christ (John 14:1), based upon everything He has said to us about Himself in His Word. In addition, in this context of Ephesians, *faith* communicates the idea of belief in God's power and His promises to do all that He said He would do in order to keep us safe from enemy assaults (Eph. 6:10–13). Peter O'Brien points out that believers lay "hold of God's resources, especially his power, in the midst of the evil one's attack" and appropriate "the promises of God on our behalf, confident that he will protect us in the midst of the battle."[5]

The apostle tells us that "above all," or, more literally, in all situations and on all occasions,[6] we are to take up the shield, which is faith. We see again from his language that Paul is giving Christians a solemn responsibility. The verb *take up*, in active voice, indicates there is something we must do in order to protect ourselves from the devil. *Take up* is a military term, the same one used in verse 13 of this chapter, and it lays upon us the necessity of completely trusting God, His Word, and His ability to help us at all times. If we are to stand strong, we must regularly take up the shield of faith and never put it down. We are to habitually trust in the Lord, who is a shield about us (Gen. 15:1), and believe all that He has said to us in Scripture. Only then will we be greatly protected from the devil's attacks against us.

In truth, the devil cannot touch the believer who exercises faith in this way. Try as he will, Satan cannot penetrate this defense. The Dutch Reformer Wilhelmus à Brakel (1635–1711) writes insightfully in his magnum opus, *The Christian's Reasonable Service*, about the devil's attempts to damage us spiritually by hindering our faith. The devil knows, he observes,

> that *faith* is the fountainhead of spiritual life, and he therefore seeks to obscure faith in all its activity. He suddenly interjects irrational suggestions, such as, "Is all this in truth? Is not all

---

5. O'Brien, *Letter to the Ephesians*, 479–80.

6. For a discussion on how best to understand this prepositional phase in the original language, see Arnold, *Exegetical Commentary*, 456.

this imagination?" He will then continually stir you up to mentally reflect upon these suggestions and to search them out. If we then begin to listen, he gets hold of us and begins to present arguments upon which he demands an answer. And if he gets you that far that you begin to respond by reasoning, he will proceed with his argumentation and will, time and again, present new proofs. When the ability to reason fails, he then proceeds to bring you from fleeting atheistic thoughts to embrace atheism itself. You will then be grievously caught in the net and be incapable of having either comfort or peace, and will not be able to be encouraged in whatever you are doing. Therefore, be on your guard against giving heed to these initial fleeting interjections. Let them pass by, and proceed as before, relying upon the word of God.[7]

FAITH TESTED

From the beginning, Satan has sown doubt into people's hearts in an effort to undermine what God has said. In the early pages of Genesis, as we discussed in chapter 3, the devil appeared to the first man and woman and attacked their trust in God: "Has God indeed said, 'You shall not eat of every tree of the garden'?" (Gen. 3:1). Do you see how diabolical this foe is? The devil, with his poisonous proposal, brought uncertainty into the hearts and minds of our first parents and tempted them to unbelief. Much like the postmodernists and theological liberals of our day, Satan tempts us with cunning questions, endeavoring to engender skepticism about God, His goodness, His truth, and His gospel. When confronted with such pernicious ideas, we must say with our Lord Jesus when He was tempted by the devil, "Away with you, Satan!" (Matt. 4:10). Matthew Henry comments on Genesis 3:1:

> See here, That is the subtlety of Satan to blemish the reputation of the divine law as uncertain or unreasonable, and so to draw

---

7. Wilhelmus à Brakel, *The Christian's Reasonable Service* (Grand Rapids: Reformation Heritage Books, 1995), 4:237–38.

people to sin; and that it is therefore our wisdom to keep up a firm belief of, and a high respect for, the command of God. Has God said, "You shall not lie, nor take his name in vain, nor be drunk," etc.? "Yes, I am sure he has, and it is well said, and by his grace I will abide by it, whatever the tempter suggests to the contrary."[8]

Believer, are you getting a sense of what you must do in spiritual battle? Do you see how faith works to protect you? The devil would love nothing more than to lead you from God, and if he can take you even slightly off course in your trust in the Lord, then the consequences will be terrible. Unbelief will weaken you before the enemy will. Therefore, keep your faith active in God. As William Gurnall says, "Keep your faith and it will keep you and all your other graces. You stand by faith; if that fails, you fall. Where will you be then but under your enemies' feet? Be aware of any potential danger to your faith; be like that Grecian captain who, when he was knocked down in battle, asked as soon as he regained consciousness where his shield was."[9]

How do we keep our faith active? First, sit regularly under the preached word of God in a Bible-believing local church, for faith comes by hearing and hearing by God's Word (Acts 14:1; Rom. 10:17; 1 Cor. 3:5; Heb. 10:25). God uses His preached word to make us mighty in faith, and when we receive that word in truth, we grow spiritually strong as believers (1 Peter 2:1–3). Second, continue in regular fellowship with God's people. Fellowshipping with Christians is a powerful means to help us keep a true and sincere faith in the Lord (Heb. 3:12–13). As believers, we need to stir one another up in our faith, and as we do this, we help each other with the spiritual battles we face. Third, privately spend regular time in God's Word. As we read the Word of God on our own, memorize it, and meditate often on its promises, our faith will increase (Ps. 1:1–3;

---

8. Matthew Henry, *Commentary on the Whole Bible* (Peabody, Mass.: Hendrickson, 1991), 1:18.

9. Gurnall, *Christian in Complete Armour*, 3:79.

2 Tim. 3:15). The Bible is living and active, and its truth has the power to transform us into people who truly trust the Lord more and more. Fourth, invest time with Jesus in prayer. Communion with the living Savior and a continual focus on Him increase our faith (Heb. 12:1–2). Jesus, our Great High Priest, ministers to us when we pray to Him (Heb. 4:15–16). He strengthens us when we are weak and builds us up in times of testing (Heb. 2:17–18). Fifth, strive to keep a good conscience in all areas of life, so that nothing will come between you and the Lord (Acts 24:16). A bad conscience is a huge hindrance to faith in God. If we have a severed relationship with Him for any reason, we must quickly repent and turn back to Him so that we will not drift into despair and disbelief. And finally, remember that when Satan attacks your faith, Jesus will keep you to the end because He is all-powerful (Eph. 6:10), and He prays for His people that their faith should not fail (Luke 22:31–32).

FAITH TRIUMPHANT

When the apostle says that faith is a powerful and definitive means by which we can "quench all the fiery darts of the wicked one," he is sounding a deeply encouraging note. The assaults of the enemy are often brutal and relentless. However, faith is our impenetrable covering. He says that a true trust in the living God will most surely put out anything the enemy sends our way. He says that a genuine faith that looks to Christ for help in time of conflict utterly nullifies not just some of Satan's attacks but all of them, without exception.

Paul compares these attacks of the enemy to fiery darts. He again draws this language from ancient warfare. In those days, archers wrapped arrows in cloth and dipped them in pitch, set them ablaze, and shot them at their enemies. These "darts" produced fear in opponents and burned or seriously injured them. Any flaming darts that missed their targets could easily start fires close by, which would distract from the battle, hinder movement, and inflict collateral and human damage. Clearly, it was important that these flaming missiles be extinguished quickly.

Spiritually speaking, the fiery darts of Satan represent every type of assault from our vicious foe. Like the arrows of soldiers, these satanic arrows often come to us unexpectedly. They come suddenly, with great speed, and often in great number. Sometimes we are even attacked while having some of the most holy thoughts about God! Suddenly, at times like these, we find ourselves ambushed with a barrage of demonic ideas. These attacks of the evil one include unholy thoughts, temptations, blasphemies, fear, false teachings, oppression, doubt, despair, discouragement, distrust, discontentment, worry, envy, pride, and atheism, which are all meant to consume us and ultimately wipe us out.

According to Paul, however, an essential way to meet such warfare and triumph over it is by taking up the shield of faith. He says that a true faith not only repels these deadly darts but also effectively douses and destroys them—all of them. A true belief in God not only protects us from being scorched spiritually but also empowers our souls to resist demonic suggestions, so that like broken arrows they will fall harmlessly to the ground. Once again, Spurgeon emphasizes this in his sermon on Ephesians 6:16:

> Faith protects the whole man. Let the assault of Satan be against the head, let him try to deceive us with unsettled notions in theology, let him tempt us to doubt those things which are verily received among us; a full faith in Christ preserves us against dangerous heresies, and enables us to hold fast those things which we have received, which we have been taught, and have learned, and have made our own by experience. Unsettledness in notion generally springs from a weakness of faith. A man that has strong faith in Christ, has got a hand that gets such a grip of the doctrines of grace, that you could not unclasp it, do what you would. *He* knows what he has believed. *He* understands what he has received. *He* could not and would not give up what he knows to be the truth of God, though all the schemes that men devise should assail him with their most treacherous art.

While faith will guard the head, it will also guard the heart. When temptation to love the world comes in, then faith holds up thoughts of the future and confidence of the reward that awaits the people of God, and enables the Christian to esteem the reproach of Christ greater riches than all the treasures of Egypt, and so the heart is protected. Then when the enemy makes his cut at the sword-arm of a Christian, to disable him, if possible, from future service, faith protects to the arm like a shield, and he is able to do exploits for his Master, and go forth, still conquering, and to conquer, in the name of him that hath loved us.[10]

As Christian warriors, we stand strong against the enemy of our souls by wholly trusting in the Lord in all things. Such faith protects us from the blows struck by the adversary and plays a critical role in our spiritual warfare. For that reason, when Satan strikes we are to look away from ourselves to Jesus, lay hold of His Word, and say with the apostle Paul, "I believe God that it will be just as it was told me" (Acts 27:25). May it be that in the day of difficulty we will do this. May it be that when the enemy comes in like a flood, we will take up the shield of faith, reject doubts, and cast off unbelief so that we will not be injured in the time of trial.

FOR REFLECTION AND DISCUSSION

1. There are many popular definitions of *faith*. How would you define *faith* after reading this chapter?

2. In what ways and in what areas of your life has the devil tried to weaken your trust in God and His Word?

3. What are some areas in your life where your shield seems broken? Are some darts getting through? Are there some holes that need mending? How will you mend them?

4. Can you recall a time in your life when the shield of faith effectively protected you? What darts were thrown in that situation, and how did a true faith in the living God and His truth extinguish them?

---

10. Spurgeon, *Faith in All*, 60–61.

CHAPTER 9

The Helmet of Salvation

And take the helmet of salvation...
—EPHESIANS 6:17

Savanna Haworth knows the value of a helmet. While riding her bike to school, the eleven-year-old was gliding downhill and attempted to maneuver around a cluster of people. As she tried to squeeze by, her handlebar grazed a wall on her right. Losing control, she fell into the street, immediately in the path of an oncoming car. Unable to avoid her, the vehicle rolled over her head. Amazingly, the ending was a happy one—but not for her helmet. It was crushed, but her head was not. Savanna returned to school twenty-four hours after the ordeal with only a plaster cast on her arm.[1]

A good helmet is an invaluable piece of equipment. Properly worn, it protects the head, a most vulnerable and vital part of our bodies. Soldiers in the thick of battle certainly need one, for without it any blow to the head would be debilitating, if not fatal. Commentators tell us that the helmets worn in ancient warfare were either leather or metal and were designed to protect soldiers' heads from blows by swords or clubs. These helmets included "plates to protect the cheeks, a band for the forehead, and a collar-like projection to protect the back of the neck."[2]

---

1. Daily Mail Reporter, "Miraculous Escape as Schoolgirl Walks Away Unhurt after Car Runs over Her Head," *Mail Online.com*, July 4, 2008, http://www.dailymail.co.uk/news/article-1031857/Miraculous-escape-schoolgirl-walks-away-unhurt-car-runs-HEAD.html.

2. Edward Hastings, ed., *The Speaker's Bible* (Grand Rapids: Baker, 1987), 425.

WHY WEAR THE HELMET OF SALVATION?

The apostle begins verse 17 with the little conjunction "and," which tells us that this phrase is connected to what went before. Specifically in verse 16, Paul commanded Christians to take up the shield of faith, but he does not stop there. When Paul calls us to "take up the helmet of salvation," he draws a new spiritual analogy between the battle helmet and the helmet employed in spiritual warfare. The analogy is this: *as the soldier's helmet protected his head in battle against enemy fire, so the helmet of salvation spiritually protects our minds against Satan's attacks.*

The mind is a major battlefield in spiritual warfare; such references as 2 Corinthians 4:4; 10:1–6; and 11:3 highlight this truth. The Baptist theologian Andrew Fuller concurred: "The language of inspiration, it must be allowed, not only represents the devil as a real intelligent agent, but describes him as having an influence on the human mind."[3] Shooting his flaming arrows into the abode of our thoughts, Satan seeks to confuse, discourage, and ignite all manner of evil in us. Therefore, wearing a spiritual helmet to cover our minds is of utmost importance.[4]

Our mind is the center of our thought life, from which all our corresponding behavior springs. Given the vital importance of this war zone, we must diligently wear a helmet, for if Satan can tamper with our minds, he can tamper with our lives. If he can meddle with our thinking, he can meddle with us, for as a man thinks in his heart, "so is he" (Prov. 23:7).

Paul tells us to "take" the helmet of salvation. The sense of the verb *take* in this context is, as many writers note, "to receive." It pictures us accepting this piece of the armor as a gift from God. Even

---

3. Andrew Fuller, "On the Influence of Satan upon the Human Mind," in *The Complete Works of Andrew Fuller* (Harrisonburg, Va.: Sprinkle Publications, 1988), 3:611. Andrew Fuller (1754–1815) was the founding father of the English Baptist Missionary Society.

4. It seems likely that while Paul's helmet allusion refers to what the soldiers in his day wore, he was also borrowing his metaphor from Isaiah 59:17: "He put on righteousness as a breastplate, and a helmet of salvation on His head."

as a soldier in a physical war girds himself with body armor and an officer in charge hands him his helmet and sword, so it is with the helmet of salvation. Our loving and kind heavenly Father in grace furnishes His soldiers with this protection. In love, God bestows the helmet, as if to say, "Welcome it, and wear it constantly." If we would be successful over Satan's seditions, we must do exactly that.

WHAT IS THE HELMET OF SALVATION?

The word for "helmet" in this text is a compound word in the original language, comprised of a preposition that is prefixed to a noun, and refers literally to that which is around or encircles the head. Paul uses this word figuratively to refer to "the helmet of salvation," or, more literally, the helmet which is salvation. How are we to understand this phrase? Since Paul was writing to people who were already saved, what aspects of their salvation does he want them to have always surrounding their thinking? To answer this we must remember that Scripture depicts our salvation in three ways: that which is past, that which is present, and that which is future.

1. That which is past—If we are true believers, then God in free, unmerited grace has saved us. He has delivered us from the penalty of our sins once for all time the moment we believed on the Lord Jesus Christ alone for our salvation, which is justification. At a definitive point of time in the past, when we trusted in Christ after we heard the gospel, we were legally declared not guilty in God's sight, given the righteousness of Christ, and forever sealed with the Holy Spirit of promise. Nothing can ever change these facts—glory be to God (Rom. 3:24; 4:5–8; 5:1, 9; 8:1; Eph. 1:13)![5]

2. That which is present—The Bible also presents our salvation as ongoing. From the day God saved us, He has been graciously changing and renewing our hearts and our character, which is sanctification. He is progressively delivering

---

5. For other passages of Scripture that emphasize the past aspects of our salvation, see John 5:24; Acts 16:30–31; Romans 10:9–10; Colossians 1:13; 2:13; Titus 3:4–5.

us from sin and evil by His working in us through the Spirit and by our working in concert with Him (Rom. 6:11–14; 8:13; Eph. 4:20–24; Phil. 2:12–13). We are a work in progress, in which God is slowly but surely conforming us more and more into the image of His blessed Son (Rom. 8:29; 2 Cor. 3:18). We are, as Paul says in 1 Corinthians 1:18, being saved by the power of God.[6]

3. That which is future—The work of salvation, which began when we first believed and continues through the entirety of our lives, will one day be completed. "Moreover whom He predestined, these He also called; whom He called, these He also justified; and whom He justified, these He also glorified" (Rom. 8:30). In the future, when either Christ returns or we die and go to be with Him, we will be perfected, having no spot or wrinkle or any such thing, which is glorification. In heaven, the work started on earth will be finished (Rom. 8:23; 1 Cor. 15:54; Eph. 5:27; Phil. 3:20–21; Heb. 9:28; 12:23; 1 John 3:2; Jude 24). In that glorified state, we will reign with Christ and enjoy our God forever and ever. In that condition, all of our troubles from Satan (and sin) will be over. O Lord, haste the day![7]

HOW DOES THE HELMET OF SALVATION PROTECT US?

It seems that Paul especially has this third facet of salvation in view when he calls us to put on the helmet of salvation. While he certainly wants us to be cognizant of all that God has done and is doing for us in Christ, he now directs our thoughts toward the final aspect of our deliverance. His point is that to fight well *now* we must always be mindful of the *future*.

---

6. For other passages of Scripture that emphasize the present aspects of our salvation, see 1 Corinthians 1:30; 2 Corinthians 2:15; Ephesians 5:25–27; Philippians 1:6; 1 Thessalonians 5:23; 2 Thessalonians 2:13; Titus 2:14; Hebrews 12:14; 1 Peter 1:1–2.

7. For other passages of Scripture that emphasize the future aspects of our salvation, see Romans 5:9–10; 8:23; 13:11; Ephesians 1:14; Philippians 3:21; 1 Peter 1:5; Revelation 21–22.

Elsewhere Paul refers to the future aspect of our salvation in connection to a helmet. In 1 Thessalonians 5:8 he tells us to put on "as a helmet the hope of salvation." Again, the apostle is clearly looking for a salvation that is to come. We can infer from his mention of hope the idea that despite all the trials and hardships we face in our battles with Satan, we will not always be combatants in this war. There is a coming day of triumph. Before long, fellow Christian, we will be in glory! Before long, we will be with Jesus! Before long, Satan and his minions will be vanquished foes, and we will be worshiping and serving our God without opposition—days without end!

What great joy and confidence these facts should impart to us in the midst of difficulty. The devil may sorely try us at the present, but soon, in Immanuel's land, he will be banished! Though at times it seems as though the enemy gets the upper hand in our lives, his day is coming (Matt. 25:41; Rev. 20:10), and so is ours (Matt. 25:34)!

Commenting on this future aspect of salvation, John MacArthur writes:

> It is this final aspect of salvation that is the real strength of the believer's helmet. If we lose hope in the future promise of salvation, there can be no security in the present. The helmet of salvation is that great hope of final salvation that gives us confidence and assurance that our present struggle with Satan will not last forever and we will be victorious in the end. We know the battle is only for this life, and even a long earthly life is no more than a split second compared to eternity with our Lord in heaven. We are not in a race we can lose.[8]

Christian, let these wonderful thoughts fill your mind and think on them often. Just as the helmet protected the head of the ancient soldier and gave him confidence in confrontation, so also this firm assurance of your final and complete salvation protects you under the relentless blows of your spiritual adversary.

Daily meditate on the eternal glory with Jesus that awaits you. Regularly dwell on the reality that a day is coming when you will

---

8. MacArthur, *Ephesians*, 366.

have no more struggles at all! Let these thoughts constantly fill your mind. As they do, you will be comforted and confident in the present struggle. As these truths saturate your thinking, you will be sustained, strengthened, and steadfast in the battle. Believer, in light of such things, never take off this spiritual helmet. Let it always be part of your daily protective covering. Continually receive and appropriate it by faith. As Gurnall says, "Take it so as never to lay it down until God takes off this helmet to put a crown of glory in its place."[9]

FOR REFLECTION AND DISCUSSION

1. Why do we need to protect our minds spiritually, and what are the consequences if we do not?

2. How do you protect your mind and thought life in battle?

3. Explain the three aspects of salvation and why the third aspect is so vital for us to focus on in the heat of battle.

4. What are some signs that you might not be wearing the helmet of salvation?

---

9. Gurnall, *Christian in Complete Armour*, 3:164.

CHAPTER 10

The Sword of the Spirit

*…and the sword of the Spirit,
which is the word of God…*
—EPHESIANS 6:17

There is something about a sword. Swords attract little boys' attention from their youngest years, and they can turn just about anything
into a sword, which is why they especially love empty paper-towel
rolls. For young "sword fighters," the best time is Christmas, when
plenty of long wrapping-paper rolls become available. Their dura-
bility is not impressive, but as long as the soldier has a shorter
paper-towel-roll sword tucked in his belt for backup, he can go all
out with the long sword until it is shredded.

DEFENSE AND OFFENSE

As the apostle Paul lists the pieces of the Christian's battle gear, he
writes about the value of a real sword to oppose a challenger that is
not imaginary. There are two different words for "sword" in the New
Testament. The first word, *rhomphaia*, is used seven times and refers
to a long broadsword (longer than the Christmas wrapping-paper
rolls). It is used figuratively in Luke 2:35 for the sword that will
pierce Mary's heart and in the book of Revelation repeatedly for the
sword that proceeds from Christ's mouth (1:16; 2:12, 16; 19:15, 21).
The word that is used in Ephesians 6:17, and more predominantly in
the New Testament twenty-nine times, is *machaira*, referring to a
short, double-edged dagger or sword that was about one to two feet

long (pretty close to the size of the paper-towel roll). This word is used many times of literal swords; for instance, Jesus' enemies came to him with "swords and clubs" (Matt. 26:47, 55). Peter used a *machaira* to cut off Malchus's ear (Matt. 26:51–52). James was put to death with one (Acts 12:2). The Philippian jailer drew his to kill himself (Acts 16:27). Jesus predicted Jerusalem would fall by the edge of the *machaira* (Luke 21:24). The word is also used symbolically of violence, or a violent death (Rom. 8:35; Heb. 11:34, 37; Rev. 6:4; 13:10) and has a metaphorical use for division in Matthew 10:34 ("I did not come to bring peace but a sword") and the power of the government to punish evildoers (Rom. 13:4). Twice, however, it is used for the Word of God (Eph. 6:17; Heb. 4:12).

Many commentators point out that this is the only piece of the armor listed that is an offensive weapon,[1] but the *machaira* was both an offensive and defensive weapon. Martyn Lloyd-Jones notes, "The sword serves a dual purpose, defensive and offensive."[2] As the soldier stood his ground, he used his shield and sword to defend himself against the enemy. As the soldier advanced, he skillfully used his sword against the enemy. The *machaira* was an excellent close-quarter combat weapon, well suited for defense and offense.

The sword of the Spirit comes from the Spirit. Certainly, the sword belongs to the Spirit, but the emphasis falls on the Spirit as the source of this sword. The relative clause "which is" identifies and defines the sword of the Spirit as the "word of God." The Word is the breath (same word as "spirit") of God's mouth (2 Tim. 3:16; cf. Isa. 11:4; 49:2), and the Holy Spirit is the divine author of the Word. We cannot exaggerate the dynamic power of this piece of the armor; it is no ordinary sword. Clinton Arnold ties these themes together:

> Paul urges believers to know and make use of the Scriptures as a means of defense against every form of demonic attack. At the same time, this weapon represents an appeal to the church

---

1. Frank Thielman, *Ephesians*, Baker Exegetical Commentary on the New Testament (Grand Rapids: Baker Academic, 2010), 429.

2. Lloyd-Jones, *Christian Soldier*, 323.

to make known the gospel of the Lord Jesus Christ, an action that amounts to a major form of aggression against the kingdom of evil. The Spirit has not only supplied the Scriptures to God's people, but dynamically empowers the words for maximum defensive and offensive impact.[3]

Although we might expect Paul to use the Greek term *logos* for "word" here, instead he uses *rhema*. Scholars widely agree that the two words are usually interchangeable and generally synonymous. The nuanced distinction is that *rhema* is used more frequently of the spoken word. It seems that this nuanced definition is intended here, so the emphasis may be on proclaiming the word, or the gospel, an act of aggression against the kingdom of darkness. Others say the emphasis is on the use of God's Word against the attacks of the evil one as we take up relevant verses in a time of temptation, as our Lord did in the wilderness (Matt. 4:1–11). Arnold points out that "there is really no compelling reason to be forced to choose between these two options. Both are simultaneously valid in this context."[4] When the Word is in our heart and mind, when we apply it and use it, it is the sword of the Spirit, the *rhema* of God.

WIELDING THE SWORD

If we are to wield this weapon effectively, certain principles should govern our swordsmanship.

 1. *Know your enemy.* Although we have already emphasized this in other sections of this book, we cannot forget or take for granted whom we are fighting against with the sword of the Spirit. Remember, Satan is a master strategist. His weapons are lies and half-truths designed to deceive and enslave. Satan wants to attack and destroy our faith (Luke 22:31–32; 1 Thess. 3:5). We must know the truths of God's Word in order to combat his lies with it.

---

3. Clinton E. Arnold, *Ephesians*, Zondervan Exegetical Commentary on the New Testament (Grand Rapids: Zondervan, 2010), 461.

4. Arnold, *Ephesians*, 462.

2. *Wield the sword of the Spirit in evangelism.* In this context, the sword is definitely an offensive weapon. We are in a war for people's souls. Those who are lost are under the dominion of darkness, held captive by Satan. Only one thing can liberate them and bring them spiritual life, and that is the everlasting gospel. The gospel going forth as the Spirit's mighty sword is how the light penetrates the darkness and sets people free. When we use the sword of the Spirit in evangelism, people's eyes are opened, and they turn to God (Acts 26:18). Arnold points out, "The Word of God and the work of the Spirit are the means by which the people of God step out in defiance of Satan and rob his domain."[5]

3. *Wield the sword of the Spirit to strengthen our fellow soldiers.* We do not fight this battle in some kind of individual, Rambo-style combat. As we mentioned in chapter 4, we are in this war alongside our fellow believers. We need to strengthen and encourage each other (1 Thess. 5:11). The powers of darkness are not only assaulting me, they are assaulting my brothers and sisters. Satan is working hard to tear down God's people, drawing them away from the faith, weakening them through his lies. How we need to speak truth to each other in love (Eph. 4:15)! We not only wield the sword of the Spirit against the enemy, but we also wield it as we help each other, especially in the context of the community of believers in the local church. Paul reminds the Roman Christians, "Now I myself am confident concerning you, my brethren, that you also are full of goodness, filled with all knowledge, able also to admonish one another" (Rom. 15:14). A timely word from the Word may be exactly what our brothers or sisters need to help them stand firm in their evil day.

A pastor received this e-mail from a member of his congregation. It illustrates this point with incredible power.

> I experienced a taste (unlike any I have known) of the enemy's
> onslaught while in the dark silence of my bed at home. Sparing

---

5. Arnold, *Powers of Darkness*, 157.

some of the details, suffice it to say that temptations to despair and reminders of the guilt within began to flood my mind. *But God* (praise His holy name!) was gracious by pointing me to His Son. My wife and fellow soldier spoke the much-needed Word of grace to me by reading Psalms 140–144 in the early hours of the morning. I could only cling to the truths and promises set out there, particularly in Psalms 140:6–7; 141:8; 142:5–7; 143:7–8; and 144:1–2, 15.

I was glad that my wife was there and that God used His Word to overwhelmingly dispel every doubt and fear. At the end, I could not wait for the morning to go to His house, where I would "hear more of His lovingkindness" and be even more "surrounded by the righteous."

In light of this, you can see how God especially used His truthful, powerful, conquering Word Sunday morning to lift my countenance and eyes upward, away from myself, to the beauty of His Son and the joy of my/our salvation. The preaching was medicine for my soul. God is so big, and He is mine!

4. *Wield the sword of the Spirit against sin and temptation.* This is using the sword of the Spirit defensively, repelling the attacks of the enemy. The Lord Jesus used the Word of God in this fashion no fewer than three times to combat the temptations of the devil with "it is written" (Matt. 4:1–11). Satan makes sin look good. He is the best spin-doctor, plastic surgeon, and infomercial artist ever. We can be hardened by the deceitfulness of sin (Heb. 3:13). We can be seduced to enjoy the passing pleasures of sin (Heb. 11:26). John Piper describes the danger:

> Sin is what you do when your heart is not satisfied with God. No one sins out of duty. We sin because it holds out some promise of happiness. That promise enslaves us until we believe that God is more to be desired than life itself (Psalm 63:3). Which means that the power of sin's promise is broken by the power of God's. All that God promises to be for us in

Jesus stands over against what sin promises to be for us without Him.[6]

Using the sword of the Spirit in the fight against sin and temptation means that we know both edges of the sword: the promises and the threats. The battle comes down every time to this: Whom will we believe? Where do we think the ultimate payoff or reward is going to come from? Will we believe the photo-shopped lies of Satan, or will we heed the threats and cherish the promises of God's Word?

We desperately need to study our Bibles so that we know what passage will help us in our own particular fight with sin. Whether we are in a fight with lust, bitterness, anger, jealousy, greed, pride, despair—and the list could go on—Satan makes those sins seem like the way we should go. Are we equipped in our swordsmanship to cut through the lies and bring God's holy promises and threats to bear?

5. *Wield the sword of the Spirit to strengthen our faith.* This aspect of our swordsmanship is closely related to the previous one. If wielding the sword of the Spirit against sin and temptation requires specific texts for specific situations, this wielding of the sword is more general, but just as necessary. Remember, as we saw in chapters 3 and 8, Satan is out to destroy our faith. He does not care how he does it. He has a big arsenal. We need to nourish and strengthen our faith every day. Therefore, our daily regimen should include the intake of the Word, which nourishes faith (Rom. 10:17).

The Word produces perseverance (Ps. 119:28, 116; Mark 4:16–17; Luke 8:15). It instructs us about God and His character and will (Ps. 119:27, 105). It exposes and convicts our hearts and motives (Ps. 119:176; 2 Tim. 3:16; Heb. 4:12) and sanctifies us by instructing us in righteousness (Ps. 119:9, 11, 33; John 17:17; Eph. 5:26). The Word enlightens and influences our minds and changes the way we think (Ps. 119:98; Rom. 12:2; James 3:17–18). The Word renews and revives

---

6. John Piper, *Future Grace: The Purifying Power of the Promises of God* (Colorado Springs: Multnomah, 2012), 9–10.

us (Ps. 119:25, 50, 93, 107, 149, 154, 156, 159). How we greatly need to be renewed and revived in this battle!

Hearing the Word proclaimed, reading it, meditating upon it, and memorizing it builds the muscles of our faith like nothing else. Receiving it, embracing it, learning it, joining faith to it, and acting on it is our maintenance program, which keeps us spiritually in shape and sharp in the battle. We must live by every word that proceeds from God's mouth (Matt. 4:4). Wielded in the power of the Spirit, we can drive back Satan, defeating whatever lies and deceptions he brings our way.

6. *Wield the sword of the Spirit in worship.* Perhaps we don't think about worship much when it comes to spiritual warfare, but we should. The Word and Spirit always go together; thus, Paul calls this weapon "the sword of the Spirit." To be a Spirit-filled person is to be a worshiping person (Eph. 5:18–19). For our worship to be filled with the Spirit, it must be filled with the Word. When we sing the Word in our worship, we are wielding the sword in song, and the enemy cannot stand. In a sermon called "Ambushing Satan with Song," John Piper recalls the story of Mary Slosser, who worked in China for many years. She used to say, "I sing the Doxology and dismiss the devil." He points out that Amy Carmichael said, "I believe truly that Satan cannot endure it and so slips out of the room—more or less—when there is a true song."

He goes on to quote Martin Luther,

> Music is a fair and lovely gift of God which has often wakened and moved me to the joy of preaching.... Music drives away the Devil and makes people gay.... Next after theology I give to music the highest place and the greatest honor. I would not change what little I know of music for something great. Experience proves that next to the Word of God only music deserves to be extolled as the mistress and governess of the feelings of the human heart. We know that to the devil music is distasteful and insufferable. My heart bubbles up and

overflows in response to music, which has so often refreshed me and delivered me from dire plagues.[7]

Corporate worship is not just a time to express emotion or to practice our singing; it is a time for warfare. When we sing God's truth, when we sing Scripture, we are wielding the sword of the Spirit in a mighty way in worship and praise.

God's provision of the sword of the Spirit is crucial in the battle. Learning to wield this sword is a lifelong discipline, and living in the confidence of its power is a faith-strengthening spiritual maneuver. May God grant us grace to tightly grip this weapon that drives back the enemy.

FOR REFLECTION AND DISCUSSION

1. How is the sword of the Spirit a defensive weapon? How is it an offensive weapon?

2. Which of the areas outlined in this chapter are the weakest spots in your sword-wielding?

3. How could you improve those areas of swordsmanship?

4. Identify at least two areas where you know you are weak against temptation, and find at least two texts of Scripture that are relevant for that area of weakness. Take steps to commit these texts to memory. How will you apply the principles behind the texts in order to resist temptation? For example, if a person's area of weakness is speaking harsh words, then Proverbs 15:1 and Ephesians 4:29 would be two relevant texts.

---

7. John Piper, "Ambushing Satan with Song," *desiringGod*, http://www.desiring god.org/resource-library/sermons/ambushing-satan-with-song.

CHAPTER 11

Warfare Prayer

...praying always with all prayer and supplication in the Spirit, being watchful to this end with all perseverance and supplication for all the saints...

—EPHESIANS 6:18

In John Bunyan's classic *The Pilgrim's Progress*, we see Christian, the main character, on his pilgrimage to the Celestial City, where he will live for eternity with God. At one point in his journey, he finds himself in a struggle to the death with Apollyon, a monster-like character that he encounters in the Valley of Humiliation. As Apollyon gets the upper hand, Christian grips his sword and speaks these stirring words: "'Do not rejoice against me, oh my implacable enemy, for when I fall I shall yet arise.' Then he gave Apollyon a deadly thrust which caused him to draw back as if he had received a fatal wound."[1] Shortly after this encounter, Christian travels through the Valley of the Shadow of Death. He notices that he is at "the very mouth of Hell." The flames, smoke, sparks, and hideous noises cause Christian to wonder what he will do, but the answer soon comes to him: "These fearful eruptions seemed quite unruffled concerning Christian's sword, as had been the case with Apollyon; so the trembling pilgrim found it necessary to resort to another weapon called *All-Prayer*."[2]

---

1. John Bunyan, *The Pilgrim's Progress*, ed. Barry E. Horner (Lindenhurst, N.Y.: Reformation Press, 1999), 75.

2. Bunyan, *Pilgrim's Progress*, 79.

THE CENTRALITY OF PRAYER

Prayer occupies a huge place in the book of Ephesians. By way of comparison, the book of Romans has 433 verses with 56 verses dedicated to prayer. The book of Ephesians, much shorter than Romans, has 155 verses and 31 verses on prayer or our prayers. Why does Paul focus on prayer so much in this letter?

Clinton Arnold provides a simple, straightforward reason: "Prayer is the essence of spiritual warfare and the most important means by which believers are strengthened by God."[3] There is a grammatical connection between verses 14 and 18: "stand...praying." The command in verse 14 is to stand. Putting on each piece of the armor explains how we stand in warfare. That is, we are to stand by putting on the armor. However, when we get to verse 18, we learn that we stand by putting on the armor, and we stand by praying. But there is more to it than that. Prayer is not a seventh piece of the armor but the means by which each piece is effectively employed. No doubt, Paul mentions prayer last for the sake of emphasis. The passage that begins with "be strong in the Lord" (v. 10) ends with "praying always with all prayer and supplication" (v. 18). Prayer is the critical component of our warfare, saturating each piece of our armor. Joel Beeke explains:

> Prayer is critical because every piece of Christian armor is useless without it. Prayer is like oil. Just as every part of an engine is useless without oil, so every part of Christian warfare is vain without prayer. Fighting Satan without prayer is like David fighting Goliath in Saul's armor. The armor doesn't fit, and it is ineffective against the blows of the enemy.[4]

We can only appropriate the armor through prayer. The armor of God does not consist of literal pieces we can put on; rather, it consists of spiritual truths that the Christian appropriates through prayer. Prayer imparts effectiveness to the armor and employs God's

---

3. Arnold, *Ephesians*, 474.
4. Beeke, *Striving against Satan*, 56.

strength, enabling us to stand. Arnold notes, "Paul is presenting prayer as foundational for the deployment of all the other weapons."[5]

What does this warfare prayer look like? Paul gives us the vital elements of prayer in verse 18, which could be translated, "Through all prayer and petition, praying in every time in the Spirit, and for this purpose watching with all perseverance and petition for all the saints."

WARFARE PRAYER IS VARIED AND INTENSE

The word *prayer* is a general term denoting a broad category, while *petition* is a more specific word. Although these two words overlap in meaning, Paul uses them together to remind us that prayer consists of much more than making requests. Biblical prayer is filled with praise, adoration, confession, thanksgiving, worship, silence, supplication, intercession, and petition. The combination of "prayer and supplication" not only expresses variety in prayer but also intensity. Paul is calling us to warfare prayer that is not sleepily rambling through a grocery list of requests but is earnest and urgent.

WARFARE PRAYER IS CONSTANT

Paul tells us we should be praying "always." Literally, we could translate it "in all instances." The idea is that we should pray on all occasions and at every opportunity. This is a clear exhortation given throughout the Bible. Jesus tells us that we "*always ought to pray* and not lose heart" (Luke 18:1, emphasis added). Also, the apostle Paul tells the congregation in Philippi, "Be anxious for nothing, *but in everything* by prayer and supplication, with thanksgiving, let your requests be made known to God" (Phil. 4:6, emphasis added). And again, in his first epistle to the Thessalonians, he instructs them to "pray without ceasing" (5:17).[6]

---

5. Arnold, *Ephesians*, 463.
6. In addition to these references, also see Acts 2:42 and Romans 12:12.

So how do we pray without ceasing—at all times? It is unrealistic to think that Paul meant to do nothing but pray all the time. Nor should we be quick to minimize these exhortations and say, "Paul wants us to have a constant attitude of prayer," whatever that means. Rather, the apostle is commanding Christians to be regular and consistent in prayer, seeing each opportunity as a time to pray.

Our real obstacle to frequent and consistent prayer is often our failure to acknowledge our deep need for God or a pressing dependence upon Him. When we do not sense our weakness, our helplessness, our dependence, and our danger, we will not pray. Having an acute awareness of the war and our weakness will drive us to our knees. Arnold explains that warfare prayer, then, is "communication with the commander-in-chief during the battle. Our awareness of the battle heightens our sense of need to stay in constant touch with our superior officer, who can resupply us and provide us with our orders."[7] Jonathan Edwards offers convicting words on prayer: "The spirit of a true convert is a spirit of faith and reliance on the power, wisdom, and mercy of God, and such a spirit is naturally expressed in prayer. True prayer is nothing else but faith expressed. True Christian prayer is the faith and reliance of the soul breathed forth in words."[8]

WARFARE PRAYER IS IN THE SPIRIT

When Paul writes of "praying always…in the Spirit," he is not referring to speaking in tongues. Nothing in the context would compel us to take "in the Spirit" as a reference to the gift of tongues. Nothing in Paul's larger theology of the Spirit would compel us to see this as praying in tongues. If Paul were writing about praying in tongues, he would be calling all Christians to speak in tongues, and not all had been given that gift (1 Cor. 12:30).[9] Not all Christians

---

7. Arnold, *Three Crucial Questions*, 46.

8. Jonathan Edwards, "Hypocrites Deficient in the Duty of Prayer," in *The Works of Jonathan Edwards* (Edinburgh: Banner of Truth, 1974), 2:73.

9. This is not the place to argue for the cessation of the sign gifts. However, for those who are interested in reading more, see *Perspectives on Pentecost*, by Richard Gaffin (Phillipsburg, N.J.: P&R, 1993); *The Final Word*, by O. Palmer Robertson

were expected to speak in tongues, but all Christians were and are expected to pray.

The phrase "in the Spirit" expresses the means by which we are to pray—by the help the Spirit gives. Jude 20 states the same truth, "But you, beloved, building yourselves up on your most holy faith, praying in the Holy Spirit" (Jude 20). To pray in the Spirit is to pray with the help, motivation, guidance, and empowerment of the Holy Spirit. Praying in the Spirit is praying with a sense of dependence on the Spirit (Rom. 8:26–27). We don't always know how we should pray. Sometimes all we can get out is a moan, a sigh, or a desperate, "O Father, O God." The Spirit actually intercedes for us, taking our inarticulate and even confused cries to God, and He prays for us. Beeke illustrates how the Spirit does this in our lives:

> A small boy was being taught by his father how to steer a ship. As the boy began to steer, his father stood directly behind him. The father knew that if he didn't help his son, the boat would crash on the rocks or be swept away in the swift current. The father did not push his son aside, though, telling him it would be better for the father to take the helm. He leaned over his son, put his hands upon his son's hands, and then guided his son's hands on the wheel. Through the father's guidance the son steered the ship to safety. Likewise, my friends, we pray best when the Spirit grips our hearts and guides our thoughts, steering us in the course that he has charted for us. Just as his boy could not steer the ship on his own, so we cannot pray rightly without the Holy Spirit. Let us have confidence in him and seek to be filled with him (Eph. 5:8).[10]

Even more meaning is packed into this command to pray "in the Spirit." It means praying with the confidence and assurance that the Spirit gives us that we belong to God (Rom. 8:15–16). There are times when we are in the battle, excessively burdened, even confused, and the Holy Spirit gives us strong confidence that not only

---

(Edinburgh: Banner of Truth, 1993); and *Are Miraculous Gifts for Today? Four Views*, ed. Wayne Grudem (Grand Rapids: Zondervan, 2011).

10. Beeke, *Striving against Satan*, 58.

do we belong to our Father, but we also belong right there at the throne room of grace.

We cannot miss the connection between wielding the sword of the Spirit and praying in the Spirit. One of the powerful ways to pray in the Spirit is actually to use the words that the Spirit inspired. Praying God's words back to Him is a sure way to know we are praying rightly. Not only is this a legitimate manner of praying in the Spirit, but it is also wielding the sword of the Spirit in prayer. Pick up Matthew Henry's *Method of Prayer*[11] or Kenneth Boa's *Face to Face: Praying the Scriptures for Intimate Worship*[12] for guidance to this practice of prayer. These works are helpful in explaining how to use Scripture in our prayers. Learn to plead God's Word with Him, praying it back to Him, praying the promises. The Holy Spirit must delight when the child of God prays the Word of God to his Father in His power. Wielding the sword of the Spirit by praying the words He has given in Scripture is a powerful weapon.[13]

WARFARE PRAYER IS WATCHING AND PERSEVERING

The phrase "to this end," or "for this very purpose," brings into focus why we need to pray in the Spirit with all prayer and petition: so that we can be watchful. We might have expected something a little more triumphant than this, but we must not forget that being watchful is a crucial part of the Christian ethic. Jesus taught His disciples to watch: "Watch therefore, and pray always that you may be counted worthy to escape all these things that will come to pass, and to stand before the Son of Man" (Luke 21:36). "Take heed, watch and pray; for you do not know when the time is" (Mark 13:33).

---

11. Matthew Henry, *A Way to Pray: A Biblical Method for Enriching Your Prayer and Language by Shaping Your Words with Scripture*, ed. O. Palmer Robertson (Edinburgh: Banner of Truth, 2010). Henry's *Method of Prayer* is also available in other editions.

12. Kenneth Boa, *Face to Face: Praying the Scriptures for Intimate Worship* (Grand Rapids: Zondervan, 1997).

13. It is interesting to note that in His darkest hour, on the cross, our Lord prayed the words of Scripture back to His Father in heaven (Luke 23:46; cf. Ps. 31:5).

Our Lord would also use the word *watch*, coupled with a closely related phrase, *stay awake* (Mark 13:33–37; 14:34, 37–38 ESV), to urge His disciples to an eschatological and moral alertness. That is, He urged them to be ready for His coming and to be on guard for temptation. The concept of being ready, being alert, awake, and on guard is attached to prayer: "Watch and pray, lest you enter into temptation. The spirit indeed is willing, but the flesh is weak" (Mark 14:38).

The apostle Peter, who was present that night and heard Jesus' words firsthand, would echo the same warning: "Be sober, be vigilant; because your adversary the devil walks about like a roaring lion, seeking whom he may devour" (1 Peter 5:8). The apostle Paul would give the same exhortation to the Colossians: "Continue earnestly in prayer, being vigilant in it with thanksgiving" (Col. 4:2).

Paul is urging us to watchful prayer so that we will see the dangers around us of which we are often unaware. This prayer is also persevering prayer. When we consider what is at stake—the dangers, the enemy's persistence, temptation's closeness, ever-encroaching darkness, and ever-present remaining sin—we must be alert and persevere in prayer.

In his Western classic novel *Gone to Texas,* Forrest Carter notes that when riders rode through the night, they needed to be alert. The possible mishaps that could occur at night were all around. In order to stay awake and alert, cowboys would often rub tobacco juice in their eyes. The burn and discomfort prevented them from getting sleepy. If cowboys on the range would employ such extreme, stinging tactics to avoid their enemies, how much more must Christians stay alert? When the evil day is upon us, nothing is more important than being alert in the fight and laying hold of the Lord in prayer, seeking His strength and strapping the armor on again in prayer.

WARFARE PRAYER IS FOR ALL THE SAINTS

The purpose statement in verse 18, "to this end," is not just to emphasize alert, persevering prayer but also to spur us on to pray such prayers for the saints. We cannot overemphasize the importance of

praying for each other. The mighty Reformer Martin Luther wrote
to his close friend and fellow Reformer, Philipp Melancthon,

> I sit here at ease, hardened and unfeeling—alas! Praying little,
> grieving little for the Church of God, burning rather in the
> fierce fires of my untamed flesh. It comes to this: I should be
> afire in the spirit; in reality I am afire in the flesh, with lust,
> laziness, idleness, sleepiness. It is perhaps because you have all
> ceased praying for me that God has turned away from me....
> For the last eight days I have written nothing, nor prayer, nor
> studied, partly from self-indulgence, partly from another
> vexatious [physical] handicap.... I really cannot stand it any
> longer.... Pray for me, I beg you, for in my seclusion here I am
> submerged in sins.[14]

Did you notice Luther's observation that "it is perhaps because you
have all ceased praying for me"? Luther knew that prayer is vital in
the battle. Its absence can be deadly.

As Paul takes up this indispensable theme, he uses the term that
we frequently translate "intercession," "entreaty," or "supplication."
We must pray specific prayers on behalf of God's people. But notice
Paul says "all the saints." We don't know all the saints! Paul is probably reminding us that we need to pray for the body as a whole.
We pray for all the saints when we remember the global church, the
persecuted church, and frontline missions. We pray for all the saints
when we remember our local church and other local churches. We
pray for all the saints when we bring individual saints to the throne
of grace. When we pray for the sick, our church leaders, the elderly,
widows, single moms, young parents, and teenagers, we are praying
for all the saints. We must also keep in mind that we should pray the
subject matter of Ephesians 6 for them. Healing, jobs, and traveling
mercies are all important, but how much more important it is to
pray that they would be strong in the Lord and in the strength of His
might—and that they would stand firm!

---

14. Quoted in *When I Don't Desire God*, by John Piper (Wheaton, Ill.: Crossway, 2004), 137–38.

As trembling pilgrims know, the weapon "all prayer" is most needful. The soldier of Christ employs prayer in applying the armor. Once we put the armor on with prayer, it continues to be a fundamental weapon in our warfare, as we, in reliance on the Spirit, constantly call to our heavenly headquarters for help, both for ourselves and our fellow soldiers.

FOR REFLECTION AND DISCUSSION

1. Why is prayer such a difficult discipline for many of us?

2. What elements of prayer are strengths in your personal prayer? What elements are weakest?

3. Describe a time when you felt an utter dependence on the Spirit in prayer, when you sensed that He was helping you. Why is it so difficult for us to depend on the Spirit regularly in our praying?

4. How could you better pray "for all the saints"? Share some ideas with one another.

CHAPTER 12

Warfare Prayer and Proclamation

...and for me, that utterance may be given to me, that I may open my mouth boldly to make known the mystery of the gospel, for which I am an ambassador in chains; that in it I may speak boldly, as I ought to speak.
                                        —EPHESIANS 6:19–20

An individual's personal prayer request reveals something about him or her. One seminary offered a spiritual life development class that was designed to explore different views of spirituality of the Christian life. It provided a time for the seminarians to gather as Christians to pray for and help each other in the fight of faith. One spring day, the men started talking about how they could *really* pray for each other—with an emphasis on *really*. Sometimes Christians have a way of praying for each other that doesn't get around to *really* praying for each other. One brother was eager to start. "Brothers, can you pray for me, because I have an intense, ongoing struggle. It is something I battle every day." The members of the group sat there, ready to hear him pour out his heart. "I am constantly choosing the good instead of the best." With that sober confession, he hung his head in shame. Others in attendance could not help but think, "I wish that was my biggest struggle!" The way we request prayer for ourselves can reflect genuine humility and our own sense of need, or it can become a falsely pious exhibition of what we want people to think of us.

Unlike the seminary student, Paul now asks prayer for himself that shows his humility and sense of need. His petitions are specific, demonstrating the relationship between prayer and preaching, and they reveal his heart to us. Paul does not set himself up as a super-apostle who has been placed on this planet to "show us the way." Paul sees himself in both the dignity of his calling and the weakness of his own humanity. His request for prayer for himself is the marvelous capstone to this section on spiritual warfare that ends with preaching and prayer.

PAUL'S SITUATION AND IDENTITY

Paul asks the Ephesians to pray for his preaching, but embedded in his request is the foundational perspective of his own identity as an ambassador in chains. In order for us to understand the power of the request, first we need to understand his situation and his identity.

Paul calls himself an ambassador. In his day, much like today, an ambassador was an official representative of a government or kingdom. When the ambassador spoke, he spoke with the full authority of the one he represented. Paul speaks on behalf of Christ, as an ambassador of King Jesus. Paul uses gripping language: "We are ambassadors for Christ, as though God were pleading through us" (2 Cor. 5:20). It is remarkable that, as Christ's ambassador, Paul knew that God was the one appealing through him. As Paul speaks on Christ's behalf, he offers His terms of peace and reconciliation, announces the good news of the forgiveness of sins, and proclaims His reign and power. As he does this, God is supernaturally appealing and proclaiming through him.

There is an irony here. Ambassadors were dignitaries. They wore fancy clothes and distinct jewelry, which signified their lofty position. This ambassador, however, wore chains. His ambassadorial jewelry was his manacled hands and feet. His chains were his credentials and symbols of his apostolic dignity. John Stott observes, "Because Paul serves Christ crucified, he considers the painful iron chains as most appropriate insignia for the representation of his Lord."[1]

---

1. John Stott, *The Message of Ephesians: God's New Society* (Downers Grove, Ill.: InterVarsity, 1979), 287.

Paul clearly identifies the gospel as the reason for these chains. He has already stated that he is a prisoner of Christ Jesus for the sake of the Gentiles (Eph. 3:1). In Ephesians 4:1, he is the prisoner of the Lord. Although Rome had him in chains, he was not Rome's prisoner or the emperor's prisoner; he was Christ's prisoner, His bondservant, and he wore the chains for the sake of the gospel. Here is the great gospel paradox: suffering is glory. Imprisonment and chains are signs of gospel dignity. The privilege of being Christ's ambassador is that Paul is Christ's prisoner.

PAUL'S PRAYER REQUEST

The first thing to note about Paul's request is that he is asking for the same kind of warfare prayer on his behalf that he has encouraged all the saints to offer up for each other. It is also worth noting that Paul does not ask for freedom *from prison* but for freedom *for the gospel.* He does not seek release; rather, he seeks opportunities for the gospel. Isn't it fascinating how frequently Paul asked for prayer for himself (e.g., Col. 4:3; 1 Thess. 5:25; 2 Thess. 3:1)? Paul did not think more highly of himself than he ought (Rom. 12:3), and he never concluded that because he was an apostle and the Ephesians were "just ordinary" Christians, he did not need their prayers! John Piper captures the reason: "A pastor who feels competent in himself to produce eternal fruit—which is the only kind that matters—knows neither God nor himself. A pastor who does not know the rhythm of desperation and deliverance must have his sights only on what man can achieve."[2]

Paul valued the prayers of God's people as a means of grace and power in his life (2 Cor. 1:11; Phil. 1:19). He shows his true humility and deep conviction by urging them to pray for him for his preaching and for boldness. Yes, the fearless apostle—who had preached hundreds of times, who often stood in the face of danger

---

2. John Piper, *Brothers, We Are Not Professionals* (Nashville: Broadman and Holman, 2002), 54.

and death—asks the Ephesians to pray for his preaching and for boldness, so that he would speak as he ought.[3]

THE POWER SUPPLY BETWEEN PREACHING AND PRAYER

Preaching is the unsheathing of the sword of the Spirit. It is the authoritative proclamation, explanation, and application of God's inspired Word. The promise of the Spirit's power and blessing is attached to the Word. Preaching depends on the power of the Spirit to make the sword of the Spirit effective in delivering sinners from the dominion of darkness and building up the saints in their faith. If preaching is a redemptive act that depends on the unction[4] and anointing of the Holy Spirit, then the unction and anointing of the Holy Spirit *usually* depends on prayer. We say "usually" because there are times when the preacher has had insufficient preparation, inadequate prayer, and very little overt dependence on the Spirit, yet He blesses the word in spite of all this. But the way the Bible tells us to have the unction of the Spirit is to ask for it. Jesus says, "If you then, being evil, know how to give good gifts to your children, how much more will your heavenly Father give the Holy Spirit to those who ask him!" (Luke 11:13). Spurgeon states:

> The sinew of the minister's strength under God is the supplication of his church. We can do anything and everything if we have a praying people around us. But when our dear friends and fellow helpers cease to pray the Holy Ghost hastens to depart and "Ichabod" is written on the place of assembly.... What can we do without your prayers? They link us with the omnipotence of God. Like the lightning rod, they pierce the clouds and bring down the might and mysterious power from on high.... The Lord give me a dozen importunate pleaders and lovers of souls and by his grace we will shake all London from end to end.[5]

---

3. See appendix 3, "Christian, Pray for Your Pastors!"

4. For a helpful treatment on the "unction of the Spirit," see *How Effective Sermons Begin*, by Ben Awbrey (Fearn, Ross-shire, Scotland: Mentor, 2008), 150–68.

5. Quoted in Arturo G. Azurdia III, *Spirit Empowered Preaching* (Fearn, Ross-shire, Scotland: Mentor, 1998), 166.

What we must clearly see at this point is the specific role and responsibility the congregation has in this warfare. Paul is asking them to be involved in the warfare proclamation through their prayers. Pierre Marcel captures this powerfully: "In us and in the Church, EVERYTHING depends on the Spirit. And since God, as a father who feeds his children according to their needs, gives the Holy Spirit to those who ask (Luke 11:11–13), everything depends, in the last analysis, on the preacher's, the believer's, and the Church's relationships with the Spirit. Preaching which is, properly speaking, the word *preached*, depends entirely on the Spirit."[6]

COMPONENTS IN WARFARE PROCLAMATION

The Word Must Be Given

Paul's first petition is that "utterance" (*logos*) might be given to him in the opening of his mouth. Paul's choice of the word *logos*, as opposed to *rhema*, may mean he is focusing on the content of what he is to say. Paul knew the Word and the gospel, but he was praying that the message would be given to him. Could it be that Paul is alluding to the words of promise Jesus gave to His disciples in Matthew 10:19–20: "But when they deliver you up, do not worry about how or what you should speak. For it will be given to you in that hour what you should speak; for it is not you who speak, but the Spirit of your Father who speaks in you"?

The next phrase helps us to see the petition more clearly: "that I may open my mouth." This is more than the mechanics of speech. In the Bible, to open one's mouth to begin to speak is an expression that means something weighty and serious is about to be said (Matt. 5:2; Acts 8:35; 10:34). The message that Paul was going to speak needed to come from the Spirit, and it needed to be spoken. This petition shows that Paul did not rest on his education or his vast ministerial, pastoral, and missionary experience. Rather, he knew

---

6. Pierre Ch. Marcel, *The Relevance of Preaching*, trans. Rob Roy McGregor, ed. William Childs Robinson (Scarsdale, N.Y.: Westminster Publishing House, 2000), 91.

the weight and gravity of what it was to speak the word, and God must give the word if it is to set captives free.

The Mystery of the Gospel Must Be Made Known Boldly

A mystery is something that must be revealed. Paul felt the weight of knowing that if the opening of his mouth was to be effective, not only must the Word be given, but it must also be revealed. God the Father must be the revealer, not flesh and blood (Matt. 16:17). Only the sovereign Spirit can open eyes blinded by Satan (2 Cor. 4:6). And the gospel is the mystery that must be revealed. Only God can awaken the sinner to his need and to the beauty and sufficiency of Christ. Only God through His Holy Spirit has the power to reveal the gospel and enable sinners to see and believe in Christ.

Paul asks that in the opening of his mouth, the mystery of the gospel would be revealed with boldness. The Greek word Paul chose for "boldly" is *parrēsia*, which means frankness of speech. If Paul is to speak boldly, he will speak directly and openly. Effective, Spirit-empowered preaching is plain and forthright. It is not simplistic, searching out the lowest-common denominators. Rather, it seeks simply to unfold the eternal truths of the unfathomable riches of Christ.

This kind of warfare proclamation has boldness attached to plainness. Effective, Spirit-empowered proclamation is always ultimately before an audience of One. It fears no man; it is courageous in the face of opposition and bold as it assaults the forces of darkness. Paul insists that such preaching be upheld by the prayers of God's people. Warfare proclamation demands Aarons and Hurs to hold up the arms of the preacher with intercessory prayer (Ex. 17:12).

The Holy Obligation

Paul concludes with "as I ought to speak." This may at first glance appear redundant. He has already prayed for boldness, but now he prays that he would be empowered to speak as he ought to speak. He is asking that God's people would ask God to help him fulfill his duty in the preaching of the gospel. Not only did Paul refuse to depend on himself for the message, but he also knew that he would need the Spirit's help to be direct, plain, and bold, as was his duty. Notice he does not take anything for granted. He needs the Spirit's help to empower him to fulfill all his holy obligations. A clear and bold proclamation is the preacher's obligation, and such preaching will be owned by the Spirit. But how we need God's help to do our duty!

REAL WARFARE

Biblical preaching is real warfare. It is personal confrontation with the powers of darkness. It involves *antithesis*: fighting the lies of the devil with the truth of God. It involves *rescue*: plundering the strongman's house, entering boldly into enemy territory to preach liberty to the captives. And it involves *empowerment*: being filled with the Holy Spirit so that the word preached will truly benefit the hearers and bring much glory, praise, and honor to Jesus Christ, the risen and exalted king.

FOR REFLECTION AND DISCUSSION

1. Do you ask others to pray for you? If you do, what kinds of things do you ask them to pray for? Do your requests for prayer reflect a true humility and dependence on the Lord?

2. What is your view of preaching? Explain how it is a redemptive event. In light of this chapter, what are some of your deficient views on preaching? Why do you hold those views?

3. Why is it important for you to commit to praying for your pastor as he preaches the Word? List some specific areas in which you can pray for him. See appendix 3 if you need more ideas.

4. Preaching is not a spectator sport. How you listen, how you prepare, and how you pray all have warfare implications. Discuss these implications.

CHAPTER 13

Spiritual Warfare Debriefing

Finally, my brethren, be strong in the Lord and in the power of His might. Put on the whole armor of God, that you may be able to stand against the wiles of the devil. For we do not wrestle against flesh and blood, but against principalities, against powers, against the rulers of the darkness of this age, against spiritual hosts of wickedness in the heavenly places. Therefore take up the whole armor of God, that you may be able to withstand in the evil day, and having done all, to stand.

Stand therefore, having girded your waist with truth, having put on the breastplate of righteousness, and having shod your feet with the preparation of the gospel of peace; above all, taking the shield of faith with which you will be able to quench all the fiery darts of the wicked one. And take the helmet of salvation, and the sword of the Spirit, which is the word of God; praying always with all prayer and supplication in the Spirit, being watchful to this end with all perseverance and supplication for all the saints—and for me, that utterance may be given to me, that I may open my mouth boldly to make known the mystery of the gospel, for which I am an ambassador in chains; that in it I may speak boldly, as I ought to speak.

—EPHESIANS 6:10–20

In military life, soldiers commonly receive a debriefing after an engagement or operation, so we will consider this final chapter a debriefing. We are going to review what we have learned in several summary principles gleaned from this marvelous passage of Scripture.

THE CHRISTIAN LIFE IS A STRUGGLE

When we come to faith in Christ, we become liberated prisoners of war. However, the battle is not over; we just changed sides. Indeed, a new battle begins within us—the battle between the flesh and the Spirit. Our former master, Satan, the enemy of our souls, tries to apply and enforce bogus fugitive slave laws to reclaim us. He capitalizes on the battle within to make us wonder if we really do not belong back in his kingdom. He tempts us to use the members of our bodies as weapons of unrighteousness, denying the new realm in which we live, the realm of the Spirit.

When we become spiritually alive in Christ by the regenerating power of God, we become aware of new realities. We are awakened to the war with the flesh within and to the world's hostility. To be a Christian is to be painfully aware of our enemies. But how aware are we of this invisible war with the spiritual forces of darkness? Ephesians 6:10–20 makes it abundantly clear that this spiritual battle is a reality. We must understand this struggle. Clinton Arnold observes: "There is a distinct danger for Western Christians to discount or minimize the reality of supernatural opponents. To do so makes us more vulnerable to their attacks by making us to be less vigilant, less reliant on prayer, less dependent on God, and less dependent on spiritually gifted fellow believers."[1]

This struggle against the powers of darkness usually occurs in the mundane. The spiritual forces frequently choose their battlegrounds in the territories of marriage, family, relationships, trials, afflictions, and suffering. Temptations, besetting sins, and struggles with the flesh are the more obvious territories of conflict. Therefore, at any point in this warfare, we must be wise to the schemes and designs of the devil. We must also ask, "What is God, my sovereign Father, doing in this?" We need to be alert to God's redeeming purpose and work and Satan's destructive purpose and work.

---

1. Arnold, *Ephesians*, 471.

THE CHRISTIAN LIFE MUST BE LIVED IN GOD'S STRENGTH

We do not get rushed through basic training and then thrust out onto the battlefield. We are called to war and to be strong. However, the inner strength we are called to is not that of a new recruit who relies on himself. This strength is totally outside of us but completely accessible to work within us. When we consider the battle and the enemy, we realize quickly we are not strong enough to fight this war. God is the One to whom all power and might belong (Pss. 62:11; 103:19; Jer. 33:17, 26–27; Luke 1:37; Rev. 19:6).

God's greatest demonstration of His power was in the resurrection, ascension, and exaltation of His Son. We share in that power because we were raised with Christ, seated with Him, and now rule with Him. We lack nothing. This resurrection-ascension-exaltation power is at work in us by the Father and the Spirit, through the Son (Eph. 1:19; 2:6; 3:16, 20). The power is ours in Him. The power is His in us.

THE GOAL OF THE CHRISTIAN LIFE IS TO STAND AND RESIST

Several times in Ephesians 6:10–20, Paul reminds us that we put on the whole armor of God to stand: "Put on the whole armor of God, that you may be able to stand against the wiles of the devil" (v. 11). "Therefore take up the whole armor of God, that you may be able to withstand in the evil day, and having done all, to stand. Stand therefore" (vv. 13–14).

When the devil assaults our soul, attacks our mind, and attempts to bend our will, and when he tries to exploit our flesh and destroy our faith, our goal is not to give one inch, mentally, morally, or spiritually. Our goal is to resist his offers, stand against his overtures, renounce his appeals, and repudiate his accusations. "Resist the devil and he will flee from you" (James 4:7). "Resist him, steadfast in the faith" (1 Peter 5:9). In Christ and His power alone, we can stand against such a cruel and ruthless enemy. But we don't always stand and resist. Sometimes the enemy can gain the upper hand. Under normal circumstances, such defectors would be hanged as traitors. However, hymn writer William Cowper says, for those who fail in Jesus' army,

> There is a fountain filled with blood
> Drawn from Immanuel's veins;
> And sinners, plunged beneath the flood,
> Lose all their guilty stains.[2]

Christ always offers forgiveness and a fresh start with fresh power and new mercies. Nevertheless, our goal is to stand and resist. We do not want to be bloodied and wounded warriors.

THE GOAL OF THE CHRISTIAN LIFE IS TO ADVANCE THE GOSPEL OF PEACE

Although standing and resisting is a defensive strategy, we also stand against the kingdom of darkness by proclaiming the gospel and praying. The One who has been given all authority in heaven and on earth has commanded us to make disciples of all the nations (Matt. 28:19–20). Disciple-making, at home and abroad, is a warfare mission; that is to say, we are declaring the gospel of peace that sets people free from the darkness of Satan's kingdom and brings them into God's glorious light (Col. 1:13; 1 Peter 2:9). So we are to wield the sword of the Spirit, step forward with the footwear of gospel peace, proclaim with boldness the mystery of the gospel, and pray.

THE ONLY WAY TO STAND AND ADVANCE IS TO USE GOD'S RESOURCES IN CHRIST

The resources in Christ are the full armor of God. As we have mentioned already, putting on the armor of God is not so much learning techniques as relying on the One who has already won the battle in our place. Putting on the armor is utilizing the benefits of Christ's redemption; it is applying His work to every area of life. It is

---

2. William Cowper, "There Is a Fountain Filled with Blood."

appropriating truth through prayer. Here are some examples of how we may do this.

We must tightly fasten the belt of truth around our core; truth must be the center of our strength: "*Lord God of hosts, secure my soul and my faith today in Thy holy Word. May Thy truth strengthen my life, and may it be expressed in integrity and uprightness.*"

We must consciously embrace the breastplate of righteousness. This standing before God, in Christ by grace, protects our emotions and gives us security and motivation to live a holy life. "*I have no righteousness of my own, but only the blood and righteousness of Jesus. O God who justifies, conform my life today into what Thou hast already declared me to be.*"

We stand firm in the gospel-of-peace footwear against the attacks of the enemy. That warfare footwear grips us in the grace of the gospel. "*Lord Jesus, O captain of my salvation, I stand in the good news of the gospel—my only standing place. May I advance today in the life of somebody who needs to hear.*"

The shield of faith personally appropriates all that God is for us in Christ. When I lay hold of the shield of faith, I can extinguish the flaming darts of the enemy. The promises of God are ours; His truth is ours. "*Lord, I believe Thy Word. I take Christ by faith; He is my shield and defender. I trust all Thy promises. They are mine by faith.*"

I put on the helmet of salvation. The mighty work of God in salvation by grace alone should permeate the way I think and live. "*Salvation is of the Lord. O God of my salvation, may Thy saving work shape and color the way I see everyone and everything. When the enemy lies to me about my sin and guilt, may I be quick to pull that helmet tightly over my head and repel his lies with Thy glorious salvation. Protect my mind with the thoughts of what Thou hast done in my life, are doing, and especially will do for me on the last day.*"

We use the sword of the Spirit to advance and defend. We cannot exaggerate the power of that Word. "*O Holy Spirit, help me to wield Thy Word aright. Empower me to use the threats and promises to cut down the deception of my enemies.*"

Warfare prayer is how we survive. We put on each piece with prayer, always watchful. We call on our Commander-in-Chief for fresh resources, supplies, and help in the battle. *"Heavenly Father, may I learn more and more what it is to pray warfare prayers in the Spirit. Make me a praying, pleading, praising soldier of Christ."*

Warfare proclamation is the great offensive weapon that topples enemy fortresses, rescues the captives, and strengthens troops. How much is at stake when the proclaimer opens the Word in the power of the Spirit! *"God of truth, make me hunger for Thy Word, and may I not only eagerly hear it, but may I do it and proclaim it."*

God has supplied us with His full armor. We are not lacking anything necessary for battle. We are strong in our victor, Jesus Christ, who has overthrown principalities and powers. He has deposed of the god of this age. In Him, "we are more than conquerors through Him who loved us" (Rom. 8:37).

FOR REFLECTION AND DISCUSSION

1. Spend time praying through each piece of the armor. Thank God for His provision, and appropriate each one in prayer.

2. Think about a time when you failed to stand. Looking back, where was the critical point of failure? How did the gospel comfort and challenge you afterwards?

3. What can you do to remind yourself that you are in a battle? Why are we so slow in understanding this part of our Christian lives?

4. What is the most important lesson you have learned in this book?

The Sovereignty of God and Satan

In his classic work *The Sovereignty of God*, A. W. Pink asks repeatedly, "Who is regulating affairs on this earth today—God, or the Devil?"[1] Many of today's Christians might answer, "Well, the devil, of course!" Pink had a different answer, and we heartily recommend his work. Is it true that God is in charge of the good stuff, and the devil is in charge of the bad stuff? Is God working hard to thwart Satan's plans and sometimes—even most of the time—He succeeds, but every once in a while Satan gets one by Him? This critical issue is one we need to grasp, especially if we are to understand spiritual warfare.

SATAN AND HIS KINGDOM

As we noted specifically in chapters 3 and 4, the Bible clearly states that Satan has power in this world. Jesus calls him "the ruler of this world" (John 12:31; 14:30; 16:11). Paul says he is the "god of this age" (2 Cor. 4:4). Sometimes the word Greek word for *age* (*aiōnos*) is translated "world," but Paul is not making a comment about location as much as he is making a comment about history. In other words, Satan is the god of this present evil age. But in what sense is he god of this age?

TWO BIBLICAL CASE STUDIES
Job

We have seen throughout this book that Satan is a real and dangerous enemy. But how powerful is he? There are two scriptural

---

1. A. W. Pink, *The Sovereignty of God* (repr., Edinburgh: Banner of Truth, 1988), 12–15.

case studies on Satan's power and God's sovereignty that we need to consider in answering this question. The first case study is Job. The first two chapters of Job are unique in divine revelation because they give a behind-the-scenes look at spiritual conflict,[2] which, by the way, Job never had the benefit of seeing. The first observation is that God, not Satan, initiates the conversation about Job (Job 1:7–8). Many assume that this battle over Job was Satan's idea. Rather, the sovereign God, who knows all things, initiates the conversation, setting in motion all His purposes in Job's life: "And the LORD said to Satan, 'From where do you come?' So Satan answered the LORD and said, 'From going to and fro on the earth, and from walking back and forth on it.' Then the LORD said to Satan, 'Have you considered My servant Job, that there is none like him on the earth, a blameless and upright man, one who fears God and shuns evil?'"

Although this conversation may not appear to be significant, it demonstrates that Satan is not the initiator in Job's suffering, God is. Second, God limits what Satan is able to do to Job (1:9–12). Satan, under divine permission,[3] then tests Job (1:13–19). God is incontestably sovereign. Satan is on a chain, albeit a long one, but restrained by the hand of the Almighty. Job then acknowledges God's sovereign hand:

> Naked I came from my mother's womb,
> And naked shall I return there.

---

2. For a detailed exposition of these passages, see Brian Borgman's first five expositions on Job in his Studies on Job series, *Sermonaudio.com*, http://www .sermonaudio.com/sermoninfo.asp?SID=910091143237. For an overview of the book of Job, see Rob Ventura, "The Book of Job," A Survey of the Bible series, *Sermonaudio.com*, http://www.sermonaudio.com/sermoninfo.asp?SID=5412167503.

3. Note that we see Satan under God's divine permission to act in our Lord's words to Peter in Luke 22:31: "And the Lord said, 'Simon, Simon! Indeed, Satan *has asked for you,* that he may sift you as wheat'" (emphasis added). In his commentary on Luke, R. C. H. Lenski says concerning this verse: "Satan is not free to assail us at will and with what power he pleases. Satan may try us out only by God's permission and to the extent of that permission—a mighty comfort for us all. God is faithful and in all our temptations ever makes a way of escape, 1 Cor. 10:13." *Commentary on the New Testament* (Columbus, Ohio: Wartburg Press, 1937–1946), 1062.

> The LORD gave, and the LORD has taken away;
> Blessed be the name of the LORD." (1:21)

Some Bible teachers have tried to argue that Job was mistaken in attributing his calamities to God. Job 1:22 rules that out: "In all this Job did not sin nor charge God with wrong."

In Job 2:3 God once again initiates the conversation about Job and then limits what Satan can do (2:4–6). Within the divinely set restrictions, Satan tests Job once more (2:7–9). Job acknowledges God's sovereign hand (2:10). In the glorious conclusion of chapters 38–42, God affirms His sovereign authority over Leviathan, which may be an allusion to Satan. John Piper beautifully concludes this in his magnificent poem on Job:

> What we have lost, God will restore,
> When He is finished with His art,
> Which is the silent worship of our heart.
> When God creates a humble hush,
> And makes Leviathan His brush,
> It won't be long until the rod
> Becomes the tender kiss of God.[4]

Paul

The second case study comes from 2 Corinthians 12:7–10, where the apostle Paul writes about a thorn in his flesh that was "a messenger of Satan":

> And lest I should be exalted above measure by the abundance of the revelations, a thorn in the flesh was given to me, a messenger of Satan to buffet me, lest I be exalted above measure. Concerning this thing I pleaded with the Lord three times that it might depart from me. And He said to me, "My grace is sufficient for you, for My strength is made perfect in weakness." Therefore most gladly I will rather boast in my infirmities, that the power of Christ may rest upon me. Therefore I take pleasure

---

4. John Piper, *The Misery of Job and the Mercy of God* (Wheaton, Ill.: Crossway, 2002), 78.

in infirmities, in reproaches, in needs, in persecutions, in distresses, for Christ's sake. For when I am weak, then I am strong.

A few noteworthy observations help us understand God's and Satan's activities. The first is that Paul says the thorn "was given to me." This is what interpreters call the divine, or theological, passive. That is, the biblical presupposition is that the thorn was given to Paul by God.[5] The second observation is that this divinely given thorn in the flesh was also a messenger of Satan. For those who immediately object, notice the clear purpose: "lest I be exalted above measure." Satan is not interested in promoting our humility, but our pride! So Satan's intention in sending this messenger was not the same as God's in giving it.

A convergence is here between God's and Satan's activities. This should not surprise us since we see similar convergences in other places in Scripture, most notably when David numbers the people. God incites David to number the people because of His anger (2 Sam. 24:1). Then David takes full responsibility, smitten conscience and all (2 Sam. 24:10, 17). However, 1 Chronicles 21:1 says explicitly that Satan is the culprit, God is displeased (1 Chron. 21:7), and David takes complete responsibility (1 Chron. 21:8). While God is not the author or approver of sin, His activity is simultaneous and coextensive with man's and Satan's, yet His is determinative. With Paul, God is sovereign over the thorn in the flesh and the messenger of Satan, although the messenger of Satan intends to harm and torment Paul for evil purposes.

Furthermore, note what Paul does not do. He does not rebuke the thorn in the flesh or the messenger of Satan, but rather he appeals to God three times. This reveals that he saw that ultimately his thorn in the flesh was from the Lord and under His control. In fact, God's answer to Paul's petitions demonstrates that God was

---

5. For a detailed discussion of this topic, we refer the readers to *The New International Greek Testament Commentary*, ed. I. Howard Marshall and W. Ward Gasque (Grand Rapids: Eerdmans, 1978), 855–56 (commentary on 2 Corinthians by Murray Harris).

indeed ultimately in control of the thorn and was using it for Paul's good. Even though Paul saw the spiritual forces of darkness at work, he also saw that God had a good purpose in his thorn. Tom Wells explains it this way:

> Satan did his worst to Paul, but in doing it, he was only able to further the purposes of God. No doubt, Satan's aim was to torment Paul—and he succeeded! Why else would Paul have called this thing "a thorn"? The thorn, whatever it was, brought Paul pain. That is why he prayed to have it removed. So in a sense, Satan got his way with Paul. But this in no way thwarted God's plans for Paul and the spread of the gospel. In fact, Satan played into God's hands by what he did! He could do nothing else, because God is King.[6]

So who is the god of this age? Who rules the affairs of this earth? The testimony of Scripture is that God is the ruler, even over the devil. God has given Satan limited power. Our response to his limited power should be cautious, yet robustly God-centered, just like Job and Paul. We know Satan has power—in fact, he has tremendous power in the present age—but his power has been given and limited by the almighty God. Satan's power ultimately serves the purposes of God. This does not mean that we cooperate with Satan, thinking that we are serving God's purposes. God forbid! Rather, we continue to put on the whole armor of God, resist, pray, and stand firm. Remember, Satan's intentions are always to harm us: "Our cold and ruthless enemy, his pleasure is our harm."[7] Nevertheless, we do not fear and despair, because at the end of the day and the end of the age, the devil is still God's devil. So does the devil rule in this present age with malice and wickedness? Is he in a limited sense the "god of this age"? Is his pleasure our harm? Do we need to be aware of his schemes? We must answer yes to all of these questions. But in the mystery of providence, even Satan is under the control of our sovereign God and king, who is the Ruler of rulers, the God of all gods.

---

6. Tom Wells, *God Is King* (Durham, England: Evangelical Press, 1992), 23.
7. Fernando Ortega, "Our Great God."

Can a Christian Be Demon-Possessed?

We cannot avoid this controversial question when we deal with the topic of spiritual warfare. First, we should define what we mean by *demon-possessed*. Some scholars today prefer the term *demonized* rather than *possessed*.[1] The objection is that the New Testament does not use the word *possessed*. Furthermore, the word *possessed* implies ownership and property. We fervently deny the concept that Satan can own a believer.[2] The preferred term, *demonized*, comes from the Greek word *daimonizomai*.[3] Most English translations retain the term *demon-possessed*. The parallel expression is "to have a demon / spirit." "He has a demon" was the accusation made against John the Baptist and Jesus (Matt. 11:18; Luke 7:33; John 7:20; 8:48, 52; 10:20). The Gospels and the book of Acts describe some people as having various kinds of spirits. There are "deaf spirits" (Mark 9:17, 20, 25) and "unclean spirits" (Matt. 12:43; Mark 1:26; 5:8; Luke 11:24). An interesting phrase occurs in Luke 4:33: "Now in the synagogue there was a man who had a spirit of an unclean demon."[4] There is a daughter of Abraham who had "a spirit of infirmity eighteen years" (Luke 13:11). There is a "spirit of divination" (Acts 16:16). There is an "evil spirit" (Acts 19:15–16).

---

1. See, for example, Grudem, *Systematic Theology*, 423–25.
2. Arnold, "The Tragic Confusion Surrounding the Word 'Possession,'" in *Three Crucial Questions*, 78–81, 138–39.
3. This word occurs in Matthew 4:24; 8:16, 28, 33; 9:32; 12:22; 15:22; Mark 1:32; 5:15, 16, 18; Luke 8:36; John 10:21.
4. This could also be translated "who had a demonic, unclean spirit."

It seems that there is no distinction between having a demon or spirit and being demonized. The terms indicate that a demon or demons control and even inhabit a person. We can rephrase the question, then: Can a Christian be inhabited and controlled by a demon? Some have answered yes without reservation. Merrill Unger, Mark Bubeck, Fred Dickason, Neil Anderson, Timothy Warner, Ed Murphy, and John Wimber are among those who have taught that this is a possibility.

Clinton Arnold argues for a view of Christian demonization that excludes the concept of being "owned" by a demon.[5] However, basing a significant part of his argument on Ephesians 4:27 ("nor give place [topos, or an opportunity] to the devil"),[6] Arnold does argue that Christians can be inhabited, influenced, and even dominated by demons.[7] What should we think of such a possibility?

Two truths must be kept together. We have repeated them throughout this book. First, we cannot exaggerate the power of Christ's person and work. Christ has triumphed over the principalities and powers (Col. 2:15). He has rendered Satan powerless (Heb. 2:14). Because we are in union with Him, we share His victory (Eph. 2:6). That union is demonstrated by our deliverance from the dominion of darkness (Acts 26:18; Col. 1:13). Union with Christ also means that He dwells in us by His Spirit, and we dwell in Him (Rom. 8:9). We are now, indeed, a holy habitation of the Spirit (1 Cor. 6:19–20). The power and glory of Christ's redemptive work on our behalf and our vital union with Him make demonic inhabitation and control of a Christian impossible (1 John 4:4; 5:18–20). Also, in Matthew 12:43–45, Jesus teaches,

> When an unclean spirit goes out of a man, he goes through dry places, seeking rest, and finds none. Then he says, "I will return to my house from which I came." And when he comes, he finds it empty, swept, and put in order. Then he goes and takes with

---

5. Arnold, *Three Crucial Questions*, 78. "Can a Christian Be Demon-Possessed" is the second of the three crucial questions (73–141).

6. The term *topos* can mean a place, a position, a room, or an opportunity.

7. Arnold, *Three Crucial Questions*, 88–93.

him seven other spirits more wicked than himself, and they enter and dwell there; and the last state of that man is worse than the first. So shall it also be with this wicked generation.[8]

It appears from this text that an unclean spirit cannot take up residence in a place that is already occupied. Therefore, since the Holy Spirit permanently indwells the believer, this can never happen (Rom. 5:5). The New Testament teaches a radical break, through the redeeming work of Christ, with the power of sin and the power and dominion of Satan (Col. 1:13). We live in a new relationship based on the liberating, renewing, and indwelling work of Christ through His Spirit.

However, we must not ignore a second truth. If we do, it will be to our peril. The truth, echoed many times in this work, is that the enemy is real, and he can gain a foothold in our lives and exert considerable influence (Eph. 4:27). How much can he influence a believer? Scripture clearly indicates the influence can be significant. As a roaring lion, Satan seeks to devour, which seems more serious than simply being bit (1 Peter 5:8). The New Testament emphasis is that the devil's influence on the Christian is primarily deceptive scheming and trickery, *not* indwelling and controlling.

Furthermore, such a belief can be detrimental to a Christian. It can minimize the magnitude of Christ's work of redemption, and we see this among those who accept a person's profession of Christianity, even though that person refuses to repent and lives in overt sin.[9] It is also demonstrated by those who diminish the radical rescuing and transforming power of the gospel. It diminishes a person's sense of responsibility for sin and can distract from the real remedy of battling our sin and the powers of darkness. It can deny the power and sufficiency of Christ and His Word. We are not saying that all

---

8. For a detailed exposition of this text, see Rob Ventura, "The Delusion of Mere Moral Reformation," *Sermonaudio.com*, http://www.sermonaudio.com/sermoninfo.asp?SID=527121443495.

9. This is a consistent weakness in Neil Anderson's works; he uncritically accepts all as Christians who claim to be, even if their lives do not show the fruit of conversion.

who believe in Christian demonization make this mistake, but these are real tendencies.

However, the other extreme—denying or ignoring demonic activity—can be perilous too. A person who lives a life of sin and makes only superficial confessions, with no serious attempts at repentance, may have an unregenerate heart or may be allowing demonic powers to blind his perspectives and influence his thinking. Under such influence, there would be some level of control as well. Again, as we mentioned in the introduction, we cannot afford to fall off either side of this horse. We need a biblical and balanced perspective at all times. Putting on the armor of God, drawing near to God, and resisting the devil are key components in this battle.

Christian, Pray for Your Pastors!

We are both pastors, and we agree that all who serve the Lord as under-shepherds need the prayers of the saints. Because the war Paul has described is real and dangerous and the devil often loves to strike those who lead the troops, you must pray for your pastors. We give the following exhortations to stir you to pray for those who preach the Word of God to you and labor for your souls.

> Now I beg you, brethren, through the Lord Jesus Christ, and through the love of the Spirit, that you strive together with me in prayers to God for me. (Rom. 15:30)

> Brethren, pray for us. (1 Thess. 5:25)

> Finally, brethren, pray for us, that the word of the Lord may run swiftly and be glorified, just as it is with you. (2 Thess. 3:1)

> Pray for us; for we are confident that we have a good conscience, in all things desiring to live honorably. (Heb. 13:18)

C. H. Spurgeon powerfully captured the spirit of these exhortations in the July 7 *Morning and Evening* meditation:

> Brethren, our work is solemnly momentous, involving weal or woe to thousands; we treat with souls for God on eternal business, and our word is either a savor of life unto life, or of death unto death. A very heavy responsibility rests upon us, and it will be no small mercy if at the last we be found clear of the blood of all men. As officers in Christ's army, we are the especial mark of the enmity of men and devils; they watch

for our halting, and labor to take us by the heels. Our sacred calling involves us in temptations from which you are exempt, above all it too often draws us away from our personal enjoyment of truth into a ministerial and official consideration of it. We meet with many knotty cases, and our wits are at a nonplus; we observe very sad backslidings, and our hearts are wounded; we see millions perishing, and our spirits sink. We wish to profit you by our preaching; we desire to be blest to your children; we long to be useful both to saints and sinners; therefore, dear friends, intercede for us with our God. Miserable men are we if we miss the aid of your prayers, but happy are we if we live in your supplications. You do not look to us but to our Master for spiritual blessings, and yet how many times has He given those blessings through His ministers; ask then, again and again, that we may be the earthen vessels into which the Lord may put the treasure of the gospel. We, the whole company of missionaries, ministers, city missionaries, and students, do in the name of Jesus beseech you *"Brethren, pray for us."*

How can you pray for your pastors?

Pray for our holiness and our growth in grace. Robert Murray M'Cheyne said, "My people's greatest need is my holiness," and "A holy minister is an awful weapon in the hand of God." Pastors are not super-spiritual people who live in a sin-free environment. All pastors have indwelling sin and are in the same spiritual battle as everyone else. Pray that we would regularly draw near to God and that He would draw near to us.

Pray for our protection against the schemes of the devil. Richard Baxter told a group of pastors:

Take heed to yourselves, because the tempter will more ply you with his temptations than other men. If you will be the leaders against the prince of darkness, he will spare you no further than God restraineth him.... As wise and learned as you are, take heed to yourselves, lest he outwit you. The devil is a greater scholar than you, and a nimbler disputant.... Take heed to yourselves, because there are many eyes upon you, and there will be many who observe your falls.[1]

Gardiner Spring reminds us,

And who and what are ministers themselves? Frail men, fallible, sinning men, exposed to every snare, to temptation in every form; and, from the very post of observation they occupy, they are an easier target for the fiery darts of the foe. They are not trite victims the great Adversary is seeking, when he would wound and cripple Christ's ministers. One such victim is worth more to the kingdom of darkness than a number of common men; and for this very reason their temptations are probably more subtle and severe than those encountered by ordinary Christians. If this subtle Deceiver fails to destroy them, he cunningly aims at neutralizing their influence by quenching the fervor of their piety, lulling them into negligence, and doing all in his power to render their work burdensome. How perilous is the condition of that minister then, whose heart is not encouraged, whose hands are not strengthened, and who is not upheld by the prayers of his people! It is not in his own closet and on his own knees alone, that he finds security and comfort, and ennobling, humbling, and purifying thoughts and joys; but it is when they also seek them in his behalf, that he becomes a better and happier man, and a more useful minister of the everlasting Gospel![2]

Pray that your pastor would daily put on the armor of God and that he would stand against the schemes and lies of the devil. Pray that he would fight the good fight. Pray that he will be faithful to his wife and love and train his children biblically. Pray that God would protect his wife and family from sin and harm. Pray that God would protect him from discouragement.

Pray for his work and ministry, both publicly and privately. Pray that in the study he would meet with God and that God would open

---

1. Quoted in *My Heart for Thy Cause*, by Brian Borgman (Fearn, Ross-shire, Scotland: Mentor, 2002), 100.

2. Gardiner Spring, *The Power of the Pulpit*, 222.

his eyes to the truths of His Word. Pray that God would empower him by the Holy Spirit to speak as he ought to speak. Pray for the unction of the Spirit to be upon him. Pray that the Word he preaches will do its work and penetrate the powers of darkness, save sinners, and equip the saints for battle and the work.

As we said in chapter 12, one of the crucial ways for the saints to participate in warfare proclamation is through their prayers. So we plead with you, "Brethren, pray for us."